The United States of the Offended

The Wussification of America

MIKE ADAMS

ISBN-13: 978-1542631303
ISBN-10: 1542631300

DEDICATION

This book is dedicated to anyone who has ever had to slap their hand to their forehead and wonder "What in the world?" when watching today's youth and twenty-somethings muddle through life.

The generation of wussies is growing up. They've been handed everything on a silver platter and now they want the world to bend to their will just because they think they deserve it.

In truth, most of them are barely average. They haven't contributed to society in a meaningful way, nor have they done anything to spark anyone's interest. One thing's for certain, though, they are offended by the world.

"I think we risk becoming the best informed society that has ever died of ignorance."

- Singer, songwriter, actor, activist and politician, Rubén Blades

PREFACE

When I first decided to become a writer, I didn't have any idea that it would lead me to where I am today. I remember back in the mid-90's, when new Star Wars novels started coming out, I wrote an outline for a story. I even tried (albeit in a very limited capacity) to find out what I would need to do to get it published. I felt like I would be able to produce a story just as engaging and entertaining as the majority of the authors who were being published at the time. I scoured the internet and located phone numbers for the publishing companies that were printing the Star Wars books at that time and started making phone calls.

If someone had the ability to watch this segment of my life, or hear a recording of the calls, it would have probably made for good sitcom content. I was convinced I could do it and had the same level of passionate determination as a child might when they proclaim to their parents at age 6 that they are going to become an astronaut. As I look back on it now, it probably came across equally as ridiculous to the poor folks who picked up the phone for those calls. But that was back in the dark times, before civilization began…otherwise known as the days of dial-up internet service providers. Before everything known to man was available in the palm of your hand.

I don't reference that time of my life in an attempt to boast that I know what I'm doing now. On the contrary, I doubt I have much more of a clue today than I did back then. I simply brought it up to show that I've been tossing around the idea of writing for twenty years. I've always been prone to exaggerate a story to make it better, but without losing credibility or factual legitimacy.

But, as the years have gone by and I've become more aware of my surroundings, and dare I say a bit more mature, I have come to the realization that this world has plenty of worthy tales without the need for embellishment. In fact, you couldn't make some of these stories up if you wanted to. You could try, but they wouldn't be as entertaining.

After self-publishing my first book, *8th Place Ribbon: A Generation of Wussies*, I realized that there is so much ridiculousness in America that it needed to be expanded on, beyond just the topic of our children and youth sports. Through the help of friends and fans, I've been called to witness some of what I can only describe as the most unfounded controversies and idiotic stories this side of a Mark Twain bedtime yarn. As the news and articles continued to pour in, it has become evident that we're headed down a path, which I fear only leads to ruin. We've come to the point in our society that has us leaning over the precipice of common sense, looking at the chasm of self-delusion and mediocrity, shouting "Hey, watch this! I think I can fly!"

So take what you read here and together maybe we can find a way to take our country back from those who feel they're entitled to it, simply because they exist.

I know that not everyone is a fan of Aaron Sorkin, but I've always liked his writing style. One of his more memorable character rants was by *Newsroom* character, Will McAvoy, played brilliantly by Jeff Daniels, in Episode 1 of the series. In the show, at a news panel, the question is posed by a collegiate sophomore. She asks, "Can you say why America is the greatest country in the world?" The stereotypical liberal panelist answers with "diversity and opportunity", while the conservative responds with "freedom and freedom." After multiple attempts to avoid a direct response, McAvoy becomes agitated by the persistence of the mediator and gives his answer in all of its glory. (Be warned, this is where the book will begin to pick up some "adult language", so if you were hoping for a family friendly read you could enjoy with the kiddos, then you've picked up the wrong book.)

Excerpt from the show from McAvoy:

"It's not the greatest country in the world professor, that's my answer.

[To the liberal panelist] Fine. Sharon, the NEA is a loser. Yeah, it accounts for a penny out of our paychecks, but he [gesturing to the conservative panelist] gets to hit you with it anytime he wants. It doesn't cost money, it costs votes. It costs airtime and column inches. You know why people don't like liberals? Because they lose. If liberals are so fuckin' smart, how come they lose so GODDAM ALWAYS!

And [to the conservative panelist] with a straight face, you're going to tell students that America's so star-spangled awesome that we're the only ones in the world who have freedom? Canada has freedom, Japan has freedom, the UK, France, Italy, Germany, Spain, Australia, and Belgium has freedom. Two hundred seven sovereign states in the world, like 180 of them have freedom.

And you, sorority girl [the girl who originally asked the question], yeah, just in case you accidentally wander into a voting booth one day, there are some things you should know, and one of them is that there is absolutely no evidence to support the statement that we're the greatest country in the world. We're seventh in literacy, twenty-seventh in math, twenty-second in science, forty-ninth in life expectancy, 178th in infant mortality, third in median household income, number four in labor force, and number four in exports. We lead the world in only three categories: number of incarcerated citizens per capita, number of adults who believe angels are real, and defense spending, where we spend more than the next twenty-six countries combined, twenty-five of whom are allies. None of this is the fault of a 20-year-old college student, but you, nonetheless, are without a doubt, a member of the WORST-period-GENERATION-period-EVER-period, so when you ask what makes us the greatest country in the world, I don't know what the fuck you're talking about?! Yosemite?!!!

[Cell-phone cameras are everywhere— people are tweeting and texting away. The audience, the mediator and the other panelists sit silently, horrified]

We sure used to be. We stood up for what was right! We fought for moral reasons, we passed and struck down laws for moral reasons. We waged wars on poverty, not poor people. We sacrificed, we cared about our neighbors, we put our money where our mouths were, and we never beat our chest. We built great big things, made ungodly technological advances, explored the universe, cured diseases, and we cultivated the world's greatest artists and the world's greatest economy. We reached for the stars, and acted like men. We aspired to intelligence; we didn't belittle it; it didn't make us feel inferior. We didn't identify ourselves by who we voted for in the last election, and we didn't scare so easy. And we were able to be all these things and do all these things because we were informed. By great men, men who were revered. The first step in solving any problem is recognizing there is one—America is not the greatest country in the world anymore."

I know there are those who consider this to be a heavy-handed tirade written by a left wing fanatic full of pretentious condescension. But I've always found it to be more truthful than popular consensus would have you believe, and I would wager that most of the people who found it offensive, did so because it hit too close to home for them and made them realize that our nation's greatness is nothing more than an elaborate fairy tale that we tell ourselves, so we can sleep easier at night. Some of the rankings and numbers may be off, since this aired in 2012, but you get the idea.

Newspapers, magazines and the internet are all full of self-righteous victims and entitled idiots.

They fill our courtrooms and airwaves with their unfounded claims and self-perpetuating misery. Whatever you think you've got, it offends someone. Anything you say can be construed as offensive to the wrong person. All of your actions are offending someone as you read this. I've also been told that my writing style could be viewed as "whiny". This is probably due to the large volume of complaining that I did in my first book. Well, you've been warned. This book is going to be even more of a cantankerous collection of personal diatribes. You'll probably be offended by reading this to yourself...and I mean that quite literally. This is your warning. If profanity laden comments or opinionated observations upset your delicate reading palette, than you should probably stop now.

If that's you, at least you can rest easier knowing that you're not alone. It's not your fault, it's simply what we've become. The United States of the Offended.

"It is this entitlement mentality that is eroding the foundations this country was built upon. The *"entitlement mentality"* is bringing down the American empire and the world"

- American businessman, self-help author, motivational speaker and radio personality, Robert Kiyosaki

WHERE WE'RE AT

I don't want to come across as an old man with my views, but I believe that things are worse now than when I was a kid. And I don't mean it in the way that our parents did when they said the same things, just because they didn't like the music we listened to when we were growing up. I truly feel that we have regressed as a society, and seemingly with an exceeding abundance of willful ignorance.

I am not an expert in any field of psychology, medicine, marketing, economics, politics, childhood development, parenting or any other topic covered in this book. I am simply an average citizen trying to find a way to live in a country where it is becoming increasingly harder to raise my son and not begin every sentence with "I don't know why they do it this way, but…"

Every generation has their share of "back in my day" realizations, but they are typically spawned by progress and technology. Thoughts of this nature shouldn't be brought on by societal regression.

Right now, entire generations are growing up so afraid of confrontation or of upsetting someone else's feelings, that they are allowing destructive and negligible behaviors become commonplace. When someone heads down the wrong path in life, their family and friends no longer stop them. They simply shake their head and move on and when someone asks why it's going on, reply with "well, that's their choice" or "they had the chance to change".

It's almost to a point where responsibilities are so compartmentalized that we can no longer hold anyone accountable. I'll look at education as an example. Federal legislatures don't want to impose on state governments. State governments don't want to micromanage county guidelines. County officials don't want to mandate to schools. Schools don't want to force curriculum or behaviors on teachers. Teachers don't want to overstep their boundaries with parents. And parents don't want to upset their precious babies' feelings. It's quite the vicious cycle. Now, I'm not saying this is the case with everything, as there are obviously curriculum requirements dictated by grade, subject, etc. And I'm not saying that schools don't hold teachers accountable or that teachers don't enforce anything in their classrooms. This was simply an example. But, in some cases, this is how it gets divided up. Everyone has the opportunity to point the finger at everyone else and claim deniability. The same stepping stones can be used in many situations to illustrate this compartmentalization. In time of crisis, this becomes more evident than during standard operations. An employee makes a mistake and the company issues the statement that the individual was trained accordingly and there is nothing that can be done on a corporate level. Doesn't matter that the issue was generated because of a dated or inferior training program that left the employee open to those very mistakes.

Just as prevalent, though, is the thought that when something doesn't go as planned or desire, that everyone else is wrong. You can find this behavior highlighted on television with shows such as FOX's long-running series, *American Idol*, during the open audition rounds. Every season, these train wrecks have come out in droves to get their fifteen minutes of fame on national television. They make it to the point of singing for the celebrity judges and from the moment they open their mouths, you can't hit your mute button fast enough. I have more than once looked at these contestants, turned to my son and explained to him about how they don't have a proper support network at home. Their family and friends obviously do not care enough about them or they wouldn't let them make a fool of themselves in front of everyone on television like this. Now, I know, many of them do it specifically *for* that reason. But that wasn't always the case. In the first few seasons of the show, those auditions were rarely televised and when they were, you could see the genuine disappointment from the *Idol* hopefuls as the judges stomped their dreams into dust. They were typically shown as a filler episode late in the season. Whether it's always an act for the cameras or if it's genuine, more often than not, the reaction to the judges disdain for a singer is typically met with anger and resentment. Comments of how the judges are wrong or of how they are making a big mistake are commonplace, as well as the notion that they don't deserve to judge based on their own merits in the industry. Some will begin with personal or spiteful remarks about how long it's been since a judge's last hit, etc.

But what may be an even worse realization about this behavior is not that it exists, but that it's rewarded. As the seasons continued, those open audition rounds became more a part of the show and more of them were televised than ever before. Why is that, you may ask?

A report by the Census Bureau shows that they live at home longer, and delay starting a family compared with previous generations. In 1975, the four "common milestones of adulthood" were considered to be getting married, having kids, getting a job and living on your own. At that time, the percentage of Americans who attained all four milestones by age 34 was 45%, compared to 24% in 2016. In 2016, more young adults (classified as ages 18-34) lived with a parent than a husband or wife. One in four people living at home are neither in school or working.

Because we've developed a society that loves failure. Being the best is no longer the driving force it once was. Instead, it's being better than the next guy. If that means you're both failures, so be it, as long as everyone knows he is a bigger failure than you. It's all about finger pointing.

And that's the state we're in. If people would start taking responsibility for their own actions, hold themselves accountable for what they do and say, then maybe they'd stop blaming music, television, movies, bullying, peer pressure, teachers, school systems, government and society for their problems. If you don't want a bad child, stop being a shitty parent. If you don't want a crappy job, quit being a sub-par employee. It sounds easy, and quite frankly it is. The hard part is getting the rest of your peers to do it along with you.

"Political correctness does not legislate tolerance; it only organizes hatred"

- French-born, American historian, author and philosopher, Jacques Barzun

Society's Downward Spiral

In today's world, there is very little you can say or do that isn't deemed offensive to someone. They may not know you personally; they may not even witness what you've done, and have only heard of it second or third hand; they may not be a part of any organization that could or would stake a claim to the activity; they may not even be from the same city or state as your or the event; but you can rest assured that they are out there and they are ready to bring you to justice for your alleged transgressions, no matter how insignificant or large-scale they may appear to you.

There are universities, like the University of Portland, that in 2016, began offering students a webpage that encourages students to report "incidents of discomfort" to its Public Safety department. They've created a "Speak Up" website in which they have asked "members of the community to SPEAK UP and report alleged incidents of discrimination and incidents of discomfort regarding observed or experienced interactions of intolerance". Aside from the absurdity of this website's existence, is the message it sends to the student body of this school. Are your hurt feelings really a matter for the Public Safety department?

The University of Portland is a private Catholic college, so there are some levels of acceptance that should be implied by enrollment. The university's director of marketing and communication, Rachel Barry-Arquit states that "The words 'incidents of discomfort' are intentionally broad as each person within the community would likely describe a different situation or experience that would define that description." The problem with leaving something like this open ended is that there is always a group or an individual that will take advantage.

In Atlanta, at Emory University, school officials offered counseling after someone wrote pro-Trump messages in chalk around campus. Steps displayed messages like "Vote Trump 2016" and "Trump

Trump Trump" and "Trump 2016". After the "graffiti" appeared, responses ranged from students who claimed they feared for their lives, and others thinking a mass shooting was eminent. The President of the University said the messages went against the university's values regarding diversity. Others called it hateful and claimed their safe space was violated. I can't say that I agree with all of President Donald Trump's views or comments, but I don't understand how any of the messages outlined above would or could be considered hate speech or threatening. But Emory U apparently wasn't the only school to become frightened by the election. Colleges nationwide began to offer counseling and safe spaces to students following the 2016 election. The opinion was that they couldn't cope with the results and needed to seek professional assistance. Luckily, all hope is not lost. Iowa Republican Bobby Kaufmann introduced a bill in January 2017 that he calls the "suck it up, buttercup" bill. In it, the budgets would be cut for any state-funded universities that spend taxpayer dollars on election-related sit-ins and grief counseling beyond the usual amount related to students for double the amount that they spend on those activities.

Not to be outdone by Emory, Hampshire College removed the American flag from the school's flagpole after the election due to reports that some students viewed it as a symbol of oppression, racism and hate. A spokesman for the college told the Boston Globe that some people view the flag as "a powerful symbol of fear they've felt all their lives because they grew up as people of color, never feeling safe." Give me a fucking break. At the time of these events, we had a black President of the United States! I'm all for ending racism, but I've never spoken with anyone who felt like the flag was a symbol of hate. But we'll talk more about this later.

At Texas A&M University, a group of high school students visiting campus got local police involved when they said that they had "racial slurs directed towards them during a tour." Are hurt feelings really a matter for the police now? The president of the university stated that there were no allegations of the "slurs" being of a threatening nature, or even what the alleged "slurs" were. But it was enough to involve campus police? This is what happens when well-intentioned plans are exploited by people who aren't even part of your organization.

Another good example of this is the Freedom From Religion Foundation whose atheist views are imposed on small towns and school systems all over the country. This Wisconsin based organization has chapters in seventeen different states and their primary goal (as stated on their official website) is as follows:

"The purposes of the Freedom From Religion

Foundation, Inc., as stated in its bylaws, are to promote the constitutional principle of separation of state and church, and to educate the public on matters relating to nontheism."

While a separation of church and state sounds fair and just, even sounds constitutional to some, though those words never appear in the actual Constitution of the United States. But it is a commonly held belief and has been upheld in the Supreme Court on multiple occasions.

The problems begin when an organization, that has no vested interest in a community or school, decides to take it upon themselves to dictate what can and can't be displayed, said or done. Jackson County School District in Ohio had to not only remove their portrait of Jesus, but agree to a settlement that cost $95,000 with the ACLU and FFRF. That settlement included personal "damages" of $3000 each to five anonymous plaintiffs. This suit was so ridiculous that while it was ongoing, and the school had taken the painting down, it put it in an art storeroom. While in storage, someone could see it and it was brought up as an additional complaint that the school still had it on display.

I get it, not everyone is a Christian, and that's fine. Freedom from religion is fine as well. I wouldn't want to impose my beliefs on anyone any more than I'd want them to force theirs on me. But imposing beliefs and having a picture hanging in a public hallway are two very different things. When attending an even in which an invocation is performed, I have never witnessed anyone coming around through the crowd to check person by person if you are participating or not. In fact, I've never heard them distinguish any of these as being a mandatory event. An announcer may begin with a phrase like "let's all bow our heads..." but let's face it, even when the masses attend their own church on Sunday morning, they don't all bow their heads to pray. If there are people in attendance who aren't Christian by faith, or religious at all, they do not have to pray with the group. It's no different than when some sporting events play the National Anthem for Canada or another country that is participating. It doesn't mean they are trying to drum up membership, it's simply a sign of respect. Respect for another person's beliefs and or practices is just human decency. Would you not expect the same from that stranger if the tables were turned?

And that's where the problem with a group like the FFRF comes to the forefront. They want to proclaim freedom, while suppressing someone else's rights. When they start their crusades in these small communities, do you think they go door to door and ask everyone what their opinion of the matter is? No, they go straight to the court system and begin lawsuits and make demands. Did they contact the nine thousand residents of Chanute, Kansas to ask how they felt about the painting of Christ that has hung in the school there since the artist originally drew it in charcoal in the 1920's? No, they simply file their complaints and make their demands. The hypocrisy of such an organization is almost humorous, it's so blatant.

You may be a member of the FFRF or know someone who is. You may agree with them by one thousand percent. And you are entitled to your opinion. But when was the last time, which you can recall, that a Gideon attacked you and forced you to take and read a Bible? I do remember when we graduated high school and a member of the Gideons was at the ceremony waiting as each student came off the stage, offering a pocket sized version of the New Testament, but I remember all you had to do was decline it as you passed by. When was the last time you walked by someone giving out flyers advertising a youth group meeting and they threatened you if you didn't accept one from them? I remember that time when I was in my twenties and I attended a football game where they prayed before the game and when I didn't pray, someone came at me with a gun and said I had to or else…no, wait, that didn't happen. None of these things happened because that's now how religion works in America.

I wasn't always a Christian. That is to say, I took a couple of decades off in between childhood and present day. During that hiatus, I was a self-proclaimed atheist. I would readily tell anyone who asked that I didn't believe in a God. I didn't go to church, I denounced my faith utterly for years. It has been over the past ten years that I have found my way back to the cross and my Christian faith. I have rededicated my life to Christ and believe Him to be the Truth, the Way and Life. So I actually have the unique position of having been on both sides of the argument regarding atheism versus religion. What I can tell you from that experience is that I was never offended by anyone else who maintained their faith and displayed it by prayer, actions or words. I would have never dreamed of taking money from a school because I happened to see a picture of Jesus in the hallway and found myself so scarred by the experience that I needed the school district to make restitutions. I can't conceive of deeming it offensive that a school system would teach the five pillars of Islam as part of a World History and Geography: The Middle Ages to the Exploration of the Americas class. But, just as I don't share the same religious beliefs as everyone who may read this, I also don't share the same morals.

No one should be forced to conform to another's religious views or practices. It's interesting that those who are always on the receiving end of these allegations are the popular or most commonly accepted choices. Why does no one feel offended by the study of Greek Mythology? Are they being indoctrinated by the study of the Ancient Gods? But when a high school football coach leads his team in prayer on the field after a game in Bremerton,

Washington it makes national headlines as engaging "in demonstrative religious activity." Who's to say that the coach's prayers weren't nonsectarian? Given the accounts of the coach in question, I'm sure that's not the case, but what if it was? Would there still be the outrage?

It seems, that these days, people are compelled to complain just for the sake of hearing the complaints. A 20 year old British woman sued Nestle because her Kit Kat was missing the wafer. Her demands include the accusation that "the loss I suffered is of monetary and emotional significance." She goes on to request a "life-long supply" of Kit Kat bars so that she can become a means of quality control for the company. Monetary and emotional significance? Are you fucking kidding me?

What's worse than a 20 year old having a hissy fit over a candy bar in the UK? The fact that it garnered enough press for me to read about it in Podunk, WV. Everyone wants their fifteen minutes of fame and the growing mentality is that they don't care how ridiculous it makes them look in the process as long as they get the press.

It's logic like that which gives us Pastafarianism, otherwise known as the Church of the Flying Spaghetti Monster. What began as a letter of satire as part of a protest against a Kansas Board of Education decision to teach intelligent design, has morphed into a following of thousands across multiple countries and involves followers wearing pasta strainers on their heads. The notion that a giant ball of spaghetti, complete with meatball eyes, created the universe is based in root on the same principles as Russell's Teapot. Russell's Teapot is a theory by philosopher Bertrand Russell that was published in 1952. His argument was as follows:

> "If I were to suggest that between the Earth and Mars there is a china teapot revolving about the sun in an elliptical orbit, nobody would be able to disprove my assertion provided I were careful to add that the teapot is too small to be revealed even by our most powerful telescopes. But if I were to go on to say that, since my assertion cannot be disproved, it is an intolerable presumption on the part of human reason to doubt it, I should rightly be thought to be talking nonsense. If, however, the existence of such a teapot were affirmed in ancient books, taught as the sacred truth every Sunday, and instilled into the minds of children at school, hesitation to believe in its existence would become a mark of eccentricity and entitle the doubter to the attentions of the psychiatrist in an enlightened age or of the Inquisitor in an earlier time."

I understand the ramifications of their argument and see why they purposely have made the entire thing ludicrous. As a result, some of these people have went on to buck the system repeatedly in various ways which range from declaring that their religious status be held with equality among the more traditionally recognized practices of

Christianity or Judaism, all the way to having their driver's license pictures taken while wearing a colander. There has even been at least one elected official who was sworn into a City Council seat in New York wearing his strainer.

The official website of the Pastafarians even acknowledges that not all of its' followers believe, but states that some do. While it is not my place to judge someone's beliefs or their religious practices, every part of this group screams of being a means for people to attract press when they otherwise would have none, and that is the world we live in today. Anything you can do to make a headline is considered revolutionary and thought-provoking. When quite honestly the majority of it is nothing but horse shit.

While the churches involving egg and flour based edibles takes aim at religion and religious groups, Vermin Love Supreme claims a piece of the political landscape. Vermin is known for wearing a rain boot on his head as a hat and carrying around a three foot toothbrush. He has been a part of every presidential election in the state of New Hampshire since 2004, including 2016 where he finished fourth in the Democratic primaries.

Known as a performance artist, it may not seem as ridiculous to have Vermin pandering to cameramen for airtime, but people are voting for him. This is a dark and dangerous road for voters to take, throwing votes away for a guy who is obviously running a joke campaign. Just in case you doubt my assertion that his candidacy is a farce, his platform in 2016 was based on mandatory tooth-brushing laws, time travel research, zombie preparedness and free ponies for all Americans. It is hard to take anything serious when faced with such preposterous concepts.

Maybe it's the growing drug use that has lowered society's standards to the all-time low point in which they currently reside. Arguments for the legalization of drug use, primarily marijuana, have become a common issue in many states across the country. At least 27 states have enacted laws to legalize medical marijuana and have established possession limits, while another four states allow recreational use for adults.

The arguments for recreational use have grown over the years with supporters claiming that there are no habit forming or other disparaging side effects from smoking weed, despite multiple studies to the contrary. There are even Presidential candidates that endorse the legalization of recreational marijuana use. So much so, that Democratic Primary nominee for the 2016 election, Bernie Sanders, a Junior Senator from Vermont, referred a bill to a congressional committee in November of 2015 titled "Ending Federal Marijuana Prohibition Act of 2015."

But, it would seem that since the majority of users experience a euphoric state and aren't prone to violent behavior, today's generation feels that it should be an individual's decision to smoke or not to smoke. This of course is in blatant contradiction to research by such groups as the National Institute on Drug Abuse (NIDA). Their findings, published in the March issue of *JAMA Psychiatry*, show that there is "fairly clear evidence" of structural alterations in a number of areas in the brain that are associated with exposure to cannabis, although the problem is not specific to marijuana. "Emerging evidence suggests that adolescents may be particularly vulnerable to the adverse effects of cannabis use," the investigators write.

The documented evidence of Amotivational Syndrome in chronic cannabis users indicates that the marijuana use itself becomes a priority for individuals, implying some level of addiction. Users may not feel the withdrawal affects as prominently as with narcotics such as meth, heroin or cocaine, but the studies suggest that heavy users will prioritize cannabis use above other activities, such as school or work. Dr. Joseph Garbely from the Caron Treatment Center says that about 15% of cannabis users develop an addiction.

Dr. Stuart Gitlow, a professor at the University of Florida and a former president of the American Society of Addiction Medicine, says that marijuana is much stronger than it was years ago, giving users a more psychedelic feeling, rather than a mild sense of intoxication. He goes on to state that daily use promotes a chronic loss of attention, focus and concentration. Daily users perform at a lower level at work and school than non-users. The lack of focus and motivation is attributed. Dr. Garbely's research adds that daily users can also suffer memory loss as well as coordination and problem-solving issues. He adds that for some users, it could change the way the brain matures and that smokers who start young are more susceptible to becoming addicted.

One of the main arguments I make against marijuana's predominantly illegal status vs alcohol being legal is based on simple results. You can have a drink or two and feel no effects of the alcohol. Not everybody, mind you, but a large majority of adults can enjoy a drink or two with dinner or watching a game and not even get to a level that would be considered buzzed. Marijuana, on the other hand, grants the user all of its intoxicating influences with just one joint. There's no grace period. It doesn't begin to work and leave you satisfied with just a couple of puffs. You smoke the entire joint and are left high.

And that's why it truly is a gateway drug. The Millennials try their best to make everyone think it's just a smoke. But why do they fight so hard for it then? Because it's an escape. They don't want to deal with the reality of growing up and being an adult, so they want to escape it all and stay high. They argue that alcohol is worse because of all of the drunk drivers and deaths they cause each year, but it's just their denial taking over. They reason with themselves that it's ok because no one ever makes commercials about pot-smoking accidents. None of them take the time to work through it logically and realize that the only reason that may be the case is because people aren't supposed to be smoking it. It's still illegal for all but four states (at the time of this writing in 2017), so of course there aren't big ad campaigns detailing the cons. They don't have to waste their time or resources on those advertisements because it's not legal to indulge with marijuana in the first place. Never mind the fact that some states report that 5% of births are drug dependent already, let's make some of them legal so more people will indulge…idiots.

Am I condoning drunk driving? Absolutely not! I actually don't think *any* of the driving under the influence laws are strict enough. I think the only way to make people stop doing it is by making the punishment so horrible that no one would want to risk it. All of these "three strike" rules are bullshit. There should be no forgiveness for first offenses. Jail time is the only real solution, in my opinion. As it stands currently, most states will give a fine, a safety course, maybe some community service and send people on their way. Suspension of license comes in but doesn't do any good. I've personally been part of a carpool with a guy who had been on a suspended license for years for multiple DUIs. The only thing it did for him was make him nervous when he passed a police car on the road. But it didn't curb his drinking or his driving.

But I am apparently a dying breed when it comes to my thoughts on substance abuse. Today's society thinks everyone should feel sorry for the addicts. In a case that took place recently in East Liverpool, Ohio, a couple was pulled over for swerving in traffic. The driver and passenger were both high on heroin, and both overdosing while in motion. There was a four year old boy in the back seat. I don't even know where to begin with the list of things that are wrong with this story. The woman passenger was the boy's grandmother. The driver was her boyfriend. She had been fighting for custody for two years to gain custody of this boy. Six weeks after winning that court battle, she and her man decide it's a good idea to shoot up while in a vehicle. Now, the kicker of the story is that the woman's sister has now begun to plead to national news outlets that the police department has brought shame to her family because they released photos of the couple, all strung out in the front seat of the SUV with the toddler in the back seat. The police brought shame to her family. Are you fucking kidding me? I'm fairly positive that if a member of my family was shooting up heroin, I'd pin the blame on them for disgracing the family name. Not someone who discovered it and outed them for it. And if they were found to be so selfish with their indulgence that they endangered children and others in the process, then I'm 100% positive I'd blame them.

But, this is the lack of responsibility that today's society has. It's always someone else's fault. Somebody else is to blame for my misfortunes. I don't subscribe to this philosophy. I think people make choices and they need to be held accountable for them. Even if that means they look bad in the process. Crazy notion, isn't it?

Accountability doesn't begin and end with addiction and abusers, though. You've got county clerks making up their own rules and claiming religious freedom. But to her, she doesn't feel she should have to perform her assigned duties because she is a religious fanatic that disagrees with same-sex marriage. Now, if I went in to my office and refused to perform half of my assigned duties, I'd be let go. There wouldn't be a court case or national news crew involved. I'd simply be looking for a new job because my workplace wouldn't tolerate the insubordination. But apparently all you have to do is claim religious conflict and you can become a media sensation for a few weeks.

But, Kim Davis isn't the only public servant to pick and choose which duties to perform. In South Charleston, West Virginia a police officer attempted to stop a man who had invalid license plates on his vehicle. When the man took off instead, the officer didn't pursue, stating that he "didn't feel safe following him". I'm sorry, was the guy waving an

Uzi out the window as he drove away? Isn't chasing down bad guys pretty much the job description for a police officer? What did this cop think was a better solution? I think if this had been me, I'd have never told the story to another soul, rather than admit that as an officer of the law, in a police car, armed with most likely a pistol, a shotgun, a Taser and a night stick, that I was too big of a pussy to flip my lights on and pursue someone who obviously needed picked up, if they were running from the cops. What happened to calling for backup? If it was going to result in a chase, wouldn't you call in an APB and ask for backup instead of just letting the guy disappear? Nothing happened to the policeman in this story. So once again, people just arbitrarily decide what they will and won't do on the job and get away with it.

Is it too much to want people to take responsibility for their own actions? For their own problems? For their own lot in life? A family in Nashville, TN is suing Amazon because a hover board they bought started a fire that burned their $1 million dollar home down. Amazon didn't make the thing. Why the hell should they have to pay for it? Why not sue UPS for delivering the item? Why not sue HP for making the laptop it was ordered from? What the hell goes through people's minds? I can't even imagine coming up with half of this crap, let alone walking into a lawyer's office and convincing them to take the case.

New Year's Eve 2016, Mariah Carey was to perform on the Dick Clark's New Year's Rockin' Eve show just before midnight. She performed one song (lip synced) and as it became time for her to perform a couple of her hits, she just walked around the stage saying that they were supposed to have a track and she was sorry. Now, I understand that at this point it is acceptable for artists to lip sync during live events. Sometimes it's due to their dance routines being so physically demanding, and sometimes it's due to lack of prep time prior to performing. It is my understanding that the latter was the case for this show. Mariah, continued to pace back and forth on stage and apologize to the crowd. Her manager stated after the fact that he believed ABC wanted to generate a viral video at all costs and purposely declined to go to commercial when the "technical difficulties" occurred. The music played, the background dancers did their routine, including some interactions with Mariah and some light background vocals. The songs were ones that made Mariah famous. Even if she couldn't quite hit the high notes as well as she once did, why couldn't she sing at all? She claimed there was supposed to be a track, and I assume that means she planned on lip syncing. But the track was without vocals, and more of a karaoke style track. So why couldn't she sing her own songs? Could she not remember the words? Was she intoxicated or high? I just can't fathom the audacity to be asked to perform, to show up and then when you are on stage and need to actually perform, that you get offended and blame it on a technical malfunction. I've sang live before. Sometimes you can't hear yourself in the monitors. You listen to the music, find your beat and plow through hoping for the best. You don't make up excuses and refuse to sing while the music plays on and dancers surround you. But, once again, it comes down to accountability…or the lack thereof.

One of the most talked about incidents of 2016 was a prime example of the lack of accountability, at least in my opinion. On May 28, 2016 a four year old boy climbed into the gorilla enclosure at the Cincinnati Zoo. The gorilla appeared to take the boy under his protection, but was ultimately put down by zookeepers in the attempt to save the boy. It was tragic all around. A horrific experience for the toddler to suffer through, both mentally and physically and a terrible tragedy that the animal had to be killed. I am not going to debate whether it was right or wrong to take the animal's life. It was believed by zookeepers that a tranquilizer would have taken too long to go into effect and that it may have enraged the gorilla to the point of harming the child.

No, where I think this story went wrong was when the mother blamed the Zoo for the incident. Everyone with a child knows how quickly they can get into something or get away from you. It starts as soon as they are old enough to walk. So anyone with a four year old should definitely be aware. I think the family should be sent a bill for the cost of the gorilla. Estimate its life expectancy, how long the zoo has had it, all the hours and resources they've put into caring for it over the years and add in how many estimated visitors they anticipate would have come to the zoo to visit the gorilla enclosure while it was still alive. Send the family the bill and take them to court if needed. The needless death of this majestic animal, Harambe, happened because these parents weren't able to keep control of their little boy. In the 38 years the enclosure was open to the public there had never been an incident until this one.

I'm not perfect and I have had my share of days where I probably wasn't the best parent on the planet. But you figure out a way on the days and in the moments when it counts. My son was never in danger when I was in charge. He certainly was never left to run wild at a zoo or climb on the fence of an enclosure. Did I keep my eyes on him every second of every trip out of the house? No. But I also raised him to know what he should and shouldn't do. It never came out in the reports, but my suspicion is that the mother was engrossed in her phone and simply not paying attention to the child. It was however observed by witnesses that the mother was taking care of "several other children" at the same time. Parenting is a full-time job. Why was she in charge of so many kids at once? If she couldn't keep up with them all, why was she there with them? Your main function as a parent is to keep your children safe. But there are times when you have the responsibility to keep society safe from your children as well.

For a few days after the incident, every news outlet and social media post was outraged at the parents of the boy and at the fact that the gorilla had to be put down. And rightly so. But then, it was suddenly deemed too harsh to place judgment on the parents. Articles began to surface stating that social media was "parent shaming" the mother and that the ramifications of it were going to cause the family emotional and financial hardships in the years to come. The family was never charged with neglect or any other formal charges. As it stands, they have walked away free and clear from the incident. If they have to endure some public shaming for not watching over their four year old, so be it. Someone has to be held accountable. The Cincinnati Zoo is left without its famous 17 year old silverback gorilla. A Facebook group titled "Justice for Harambe" was created and an online petition garnered over 500,000 supporters demanding that the parents be held accountable. But again, no charges were filed.

Some claim the Zoo should have had a second barrier in place to prevent someone from gaining access to the enclosure. The Zoo raised the barrier 6 inches, up to 42 after the incident. But it's a Zoo. You'd think the 36 inch barrier on the edge of a fucking fifteen foot deep moat would be enough to deter people from entering. But when you don't teach your children boundaries, and you feel like the whole world should bow to your every whim, I guess it's easy to make demands for extra preventive measures to be taken. I'm sure some who read this will disagree with me. That's fine, disagree. This is my book. Go write your own if you want to voice your opinion.

But this is the society that we live in. It's a place where you can sue Starbucks for having a quarter inch of foam in your latte or for having too much ice in your iced coffee. A quarter inch. Have these people looked a ruler lately to understand how small a quarter of an inch is? As for the ice, I don't drink iced coffee, but it seems self-explanatory to me and very much implied that there will be ice in it. Why couldn't the customer simply ask for less ice? I hear people order their coffee extra hot all the time. Is this not the same principle? Why would either of these necessitate a lawsuit?

A few years ago, a woman in Georgia went to a Publix where a worker was changing the sign using a bucket truck. Cones were placed on either side of the truck. Surveillance footage shows the woman parking behind the truck and walking underneath the ladder. She goes back to her car and while she's there, the worker lowers the bucket. The ladder was painted orange, the woman had walked by it three times, but when she returned, she was engrossed in her phone, with it positioned in front of her face and ran into the ladder. She hit it so hard she received a mild concussion from it and was taken by ambulance from the scene. Seems like a case of stupidity, right? Apparently not to a judge who entertained the case. The woman sued the worker's company and it was deemed that she was only 8% liable for her injuries. How is that even possible? Was the worker supposed to tackle her before she got close enough to slam her own head into the ladder? She the company have had a team of workers surrounding the entire area to keep people away like riot police to prevent injuries from dumbasses who can't be bothered to pay attention to where they are going? I just don't understand how it's even possible to win a lawsuit like this. There is video evidence of the entire event. It's not even a "he said/she said" situation. Why is this different than driving accidents when phones are involved? If I drove into a parked vehicle and tore my car up because I was looking at my phone, I'd be charged with distracted driving as well as probably reckless endangerment, and some other violations because I wasn't paying attention. I certainly wouldn't be awarded money for any injuries I incurred or damages to my vehicle. Yet, this woman got over a $160,000 settlement for walking into this ladder.

I remember when I was in my twenties and working at a local retail shop, we had a marquee sign out front. The kind where the top of the sign formed an arrow to point toward the store. It sat in the parking lot beside the sidewalk and one time it got moved (from a windy storm or something) and I was asked to move it back out away from the sidewalk. When I asked why, I was told of a very similar story where a woman was walking into the building and didn't pay attention to where she was going and walked into the marquee, scratching her face (or her eye, or forehead…I don't remember the details). She sued the shop for her medical bills after going to the emergency room and won the settlement. How privileged life must be for those who don't even have to watch where they walk.

In similar cases, gym goers using workout equipment have sued the gym stating they were not given proper instruction on the machines, which resulted in injuries. Even though they signed a waiver stating they wouldn't hold the gym liable.

It seems every year that people try to outdo each other to come up with the most asinine lawsuits. But have no fear. No matter how dumb you may think a lawsuit is, there is always someone there to look even more ridiculous!

MasterCard had to fend off a lawsuit surrounding their "Stand Up To Cancer" campaign in which they raised over $30 million for cancer research in just five years. The lawsuit was filed by a group of folks who felt MasterCard should have stopped advertising the campaign after their initial goal of $4 million was met. Because they continued with the ads and campaign for five years the group sought "damages of more than $5 million, including punitive damages, injunctive relief, attorney fees, and costs of the lawsuit."

A monkey took a nature photographers camera and accidentally took a selfie which was published in a 2011 book called *Wildlife Personalities*. The photographer of course used his own copyright for the image, as one would expect. PETA however disagreed with this assumption and filed a lawsuit stating that the monkey should be the beneficiary of all financial benefits obtained through the use of this photo. A federal judge, thankfully, tossed the case citing that copyrights can only be owned by human beings. However, an appeal was filed. I get it when an organization wants to stand up for animal rights to prevent abuse and neglect, but are you fucking kidding me with this, PETA?

In Nebraska, a man is trying to end the University of Nebraska's tradition of releasing red balloons upon the scoring of the first touchdown of the season. The school has been doing this for over 50 years and uses only biodegradable balloons and cotton strings in an effort to remain environmentally friendly. However, the man claims that the balloons falling back to earth poses a threat to the health and safety of children and wildlife, contending the balloon release is really just "the open dumping of solid waste." Sounds like a crotchety old man that hates football, if you ask me.

In New Jersey, a nine year old boy was called a racist and the local police were called because he asked if there were any more brownies at lunch. A fellow student misinterpreted the comment and reported it to the school upon which they called law enforcement. Because he wanted more dessert, nothing more.

I know you're tired of hearing me recite ridiculous lawsuits, so I'll end this section here. I have only brought these before you to illustrate the type of trash that fills our courtrooms and legal system. The "Judge Judy" mentality has plagued America for over 20 years now, and Americans eat it up hook, line and sinker. The venerable judge herself pulls in approximately $47 million a year for the show, so obviously people are watching. But this lawsuit generation is running amuck throughout society. Companies are so afraid of lawsuits that they hamper their own abilities to prosper. Individuals are so concerned with the same that they will allow actions to continue that would never have been permitted, but they are afraid of finding themselves in a courtroom defending themselves.

As damning as the evidence is that our society is in a downward spiral, there are certainly no requirements of court cases to illustrate it.

An article by Ross Pomeroy and William Handke, published January 8, 2015, from *Business Insider* reads "For the first time in America's history, an entire generation of her citizens are poorer, more indebted, and less employed than the preceding generations." They are referring to the Millennials, or the generation who reached adulthood around the year 2000. The bulk of this particular article is a slanted view attempting to defend the Millennials, stating that placing blame on them is like blaming a victim. They go on to say that the Baby Boomers are to blame for the current state of affairs and that the Millennials are simply bystanders unable to make the necessary changes to right the ship. It goes on a tirade about the National debt and taxes, etc., but none of those things had any direct consequences on the life skills that are sorely lacking with this group.

While the Millennials may not have dug the hole by themselves, they certainly aren't doing anything to climb back out of it, either. And while I have certainly beaten up the good name of the Millennials myself, it is not entirely unfounded to place blame on their shoulders. According to a study by a Princeton-based research group, Millennials lack common skills that employers want the most, including literacy, practical math and problem-solving. Now what part of any of those skills can be blamed on past generations? What makes this so much worse is knowing that the Millennials are all of breeding age now and filling our schools with their entitled brats, some of whom will soon be entering the workforce and wreaking havoc on society themselves. Obviously not all Millennials are dumb or illiterate. But American Millennials rank behind most other countries in studies of the aforementioned skills.

Not only are these findings concerning for those being studied, but also for the future of America. This under-employed, debt-laden, self-righteous subgroup of the population is in their thirties now. They are doctors, nurses, teachers, police, firemen, CEOs and lawyers. And all of their entitlement is now being reflected in their policies, actions and business practices.

And remember, in addition to thinking everyone should be allowed to get high whenever they want, despite being proven as having less problem-solving skills and literacy levels, this group thinks they know more than anyone else. I know that's an age-old adage that every generation feels they know more than all who came before them. But in this case, it really seems to be true…that they feel that way, not that they are smarter.

For example, I have witnessed on multiple occasions in the past couple of years a situation where an organization will make a decision regarding communication or scheduled events or any number of other things, and instead of following the guidelines provided, there always seems to be a small group who think they know better. A youth league decides not to have an end of season banquet and provides the logic behind their decision. But a group of the "soccer moms" get together and decide that they need to have a party, regardless of what the league has stated. And then it is found out that 3 of the 5 teams had private parties for just their team's players. Now, you may be thinking along the same lines as these moms, that the kids deserve a party. But what happens when you have these couple of moms that go rogue is that it makes everyone else look like an ass. Now you've got three teams who had parties and they tell their buddies about them, so now the two teams that followed the league guidelines have kids that feel left out, or that their coaches were dicks because they didn't throw them a party. When all of it could have been avoided if everyone in the organization would have followed the guidelines passed down from the league board members.

In another instance a high school team advised everyone at a "mandatory" parent meeting that all team correspondence would be handled via a closed Facebook group. All were advised to sign up for it and to check it often for team news, schedules and instructions. Past seasons a separate group had been created for the freshmen team as they adhered to a different schedule for games. It was specifically mentioned that this new group was to include all members of the program and to promote having everyone on the same page at all times. So, one group to provide information to the entire program. It wasn't long into the season that one of the freshmen parents was asked a question and responded that they would get with their freshmen group and see. So once again, a handful of individuals decide they know more than the organization and directly go against the wishes of the group.

But it happens everywhere. Parents think they are smarter than teachers so they decide to homeschool. People think they are smarter than doctors so they refuse medication and treatment. Sometimes those two cross streams to form a special kind of moron. A woman in Texas who is against vaccinations was throwing "Pox Parties" where she had unvaccinated children come over to play with children who had active cases of chickenpox. What's worse is that she doesn't feel she was doing anything wrong, maintaining that her "Pox Parties" were not dangerous. Never mind that the New England Journal of Medicine states that chickenpox caused over 30,000 hospitalizations and 150 deaths each year prior to the introduction of vaccinations. But far be it for anyone to tell this nut job that she is wrong. Child Protective Services, however put an end to her parties. I get being skeptical of some things. Especially with all medical and scientific studies showing that the benefits of vaccination far outweigh the risks, it is hard for me to condone any parent denying their child of these simplest of safety measures. If you want to act like medicine is poison and refuse treatments as an adult, more power to you. But to impose those views on a child who isn't old enough to make an informed decision, let alone speak most of the time is simply irrational and irresponsible. To those who are against vaccinations, have you ever stopped to consider why we haven't had an outbreak of small pox, diphtheria or polio since the early 1900's? It's not because these diseases were eradicated from the Earth. It's because we vaccinate for them. Are vaccinations 100% effective? No, but I'd much rather my chances with them than without. A study in 2006 yielded that each of the three diseases named above had 100% decrease since the turn of the 20th century, down to zero from over 240,000 collective cases at that time (with 175,000 of those being diphtheria).

Why does this work when there are radicals like this lady who think they don't need the shots? Herd immunity. Herd immunity is a general immunity to a pathogen in a population based on the acquired immunity to it by a high proportion of members over time. Studies suggest that if less than 90% of children are immunized in a particular community, these areas of low vaccination can create an environment conducive to infectious diseases, enabling them to take hold and spread.

States that had policies in place to allow parents to exempt their children from immunization show a 90% higher incidence of whooping cough in 2011.

That is just one example of how this house of cards we live in can tumble down when people think they know more than scientists and professionals who dedicate their lives to these studies. The short of it is that the risks natural infection far exceed the risks of immunization for every recommended vaccine. You may have the right to decline vaccination for your child, but that doesn't make it the right decision. But what do I know? I'm not a doctor, psychiatrist, scientist, medical journalist or professional researcher.

"Racism is taught in our society, it is not automatic. It is learned behavior toward persons with dissimilar physical characteristics."

- American writer, editor, decorated soldier, special Pulitzer Prize recipient and author of Roots: The Saga of an American Family, Alex Haley

RACISM & SEXISM

This will without a doubt be my most controversial chapter, but I feel like it needs to be included. Too many of the headlines in today's news revolve around one or both of these topics. The problem is that everyone is so afraid to confront anyone else on either of them that they are both getting out of hand in epic proportions.

This chapter may make you uncomfortable or even outraged. Tough shit. My book, my topics. But I do want to establish right now that I don't care if you're purple with green spots, white, black, straight, gay, bi, trans or asexual. I just don't care. What I care about is how you act and how you treat me and other people you interact with. If I don't care for you it's because you're an asshole, not because of your race or sexual orientation.

The last couple of years have been a racial firestorm in the media. Between the riots and protests to wide-spread cop killings, it is evident that there are parts of the country in which racism is alive and well as if the Civil Rights movement never happened. While I know there are acts that prompt the stories, one of the things that bothers me the most is the way the media portrays everything as being a racial issue. Yes, there are plenty of racial issues that need to be brought out. But anytime someone gets shot by someone else it doesn't mean that it was a racially motivated crime just because one was black and the other was white.

One relatively recent "scandal" that made headlines surrounded the Academy Awards and it's lack of African-American nominees. Spike Lee and Jada Pinkett-Smith advocate boycotting Academy Awards with accusations of racism amongst voters because for two years no black actors/actresses were nominated. While the evidence may suggest this is the case, some of the questions and statements that were made are what pisses me off. Jada Pinkett Smith states in her video "…and now I think that it is OUR responsibility now, to make the change.

Maybe it's time that we pull back our resources and we put them BACK into OUR communities, into OUR programs and WE make programs for ourselves that acknowledge us in ways that we see fit, that are just as good as the so called "mainstream"…"

Spike Lee says ""We Cannot Support It And Mean No Disrespect To My Friends, Host Chris Rock and Producer Reggie Hudlin, President Isaacs And The Academy," he captioned the photo. "But, How Is It Possible For The 2nd Consecutive Year All 20 Contenders Under The Actor Category Are White? And Let's Not Even Get Into The Other Branches. 40 White Actors In 2 Years And No Flava At All. We Can't Act?! WTF!!"

Whoopi Goldberg adds "You wanna boycott something? Don't go see the movies that don't have your representation. That's the boycott you want," she said. "To me, we have this conversation every year. It pisses me off." I wonder if she has ever complained about winning her own Oscar back in 1990?

Biracial actress Stacey Dash spoke out against the boycott, stating that the problem extends beyond the Oscars and includes any programming that excludes people because of race. "We can either have integration or segregation. If we don't want segregation then we need to get rid of channels like BET and the BET awards and the Image Awards. If it were the other way around we would be up in arms. It's a double standard." Dash was crucified on social media by blacks accusing her of turning against her racial heritage. They were appalled by her criticism of BET because she was a previous recipient of a BET Award.

And all of this because there weren't any black nominees in the 87th or 88th Academy Awards in major categories. Social media was pollutted with #OscarsSoWhite and folks who were offended and screaming for the Academy's disbandment. Personally, I liked Jamie Foxx's response the best. He joked that he and Denzel Washington took a picture of their Oscars and tweeted it out to everyone with hashtags like #ActBetter and #WhatsTheBigDeal?

What if I wanted to boycott because there were no fat men nominated? You have to go back just as far to find a portly nominee. Back to when Jonah Hill was nominated for Best Supporting Actor for his work in *The Wolf of Wall Street.*

Sounds ridiculous, doesn't it? To me, this is no more ridiculous than the current mindset of a select group of outspoken African-American Hollywood individuals who feel that there should be a nominee "of color" at the Academy Awards. If you want to be nominated, make better movies. Jada, if you are upset because your husband wasn't nominated for *Concussion*, tell him to pick better roles. His last few dramas have been a cure for insomnia. You also can't make two or three movies that are made up of a predominantly black cast and then just expect one of them to win awards. You have to produce quality to get recognized. Not every song is a hit, even when released by a multi-platinum recording artist. If you truly feel someone got snubbed, protest it as such and don't make it a racial issue. Stacey Dash is right. You can't continue to demand things based on race and then bitch about racism being alive and well in America. Stop playing the race card every time you don't get your way. No one that is currently living (unless the Guinness Book of World Records has incorrect statistics on who the oldest people in the world are) was alive when there were slaves in America. No one currently alive did this. Let it go. Slavery was around for thousands of years before America was ever thought of. The blacks are not the first race to be slaves, nor were they in bondage the longest.

Actually, the first American slave owner was a free black man named Anthony Johnson. His accounts are documented in court records from 1655. He came to America as a slave himself, but after the farm he worked on was wiped out by the Powhatan Indians, he was released and legally recognized as a "free Negro". He went on to run a successful farm himself and owned as many as five black indentured servants, one of whom left and became the topic of the aforementioned court documentation. It is believed that by 1830, there were over 3500 black families in the South who owned slaves. One report showed that by 1860, there were approximately 3000 slaves owned by black households in the city of New Orleans alone. But no one ever mentions *that* in their arguments about oppression.

Western Kentucky University's student government passed a resolution calling for free tuition for black students as reparations for slavery. The university president has stated that the school will not adopt the resolution as official policy and that he understands using it as a conversation starter…but, c'mon!

There were slaves in Babylon, ancient Greece, Rome, during the Middle Ages and the list goes on and on. Portuguese traders were the first to enslave Africans in the 15th century. So why are American whites held accountable for slavery in the minds of every black person with a grudge? What if all of the Northeastern descendants of pilgrims decided to begin protesting anything that involved Great Britain because of how they were persecuted for their religious beliefs?

I will be criticized by those who say I have no idea what I'm talking about because I'm white. That I've never experienced racism and therefore I have no business commenting on it or scrutinizing those who have public sway or make public remarks. Maybe I have lived a sheltered life. We were called porch monkeys and yard apes all through childhood. As far as we knew it was a term used for kids and how they act like wild animals. It wasn't until later in life that we learned that they were in fact, rooted in racism and not terms of endearment.

We lived in a white neighborhood. Not like a gated community or anything, it was just that our end of town was white. The entire time I went through school there was one black family that lived in our school district. I wasn't around any of the children enough to see if anyone treated them poorly or not, but I never heard anything bad. It wasn't until high school, when I started meeting kids from other schools that I realized just how white our community was. My first memory of being conscious of our ethnicity was in 9th Grade while on a trip with the high school band. We were in Florida, and as we left the auditorium from our performance, a member of another band asked "where's all the brothers?" and someone replied "we ain't got no brothers". It wasn't really until that moment that I realized how truly white our entire community was at that time. I only write about these things to illustrate that racism is taught. I never felt it. I never saw any difference in anyone because of their skin color. I have always placed the importance on an individual's actions that to base my judgments. One of my closest friends in the world, fell in love with and planned to marry a black man a few years after we graduated high school. Much to the dismay of her parents. My wife and I were the only other white people at the wedding, besides the bride, that I recall. Her mother finally started to come around a few years later with the birth of their first son, but when we went to the christening, we were still two of approximately four white people in attendance.

One of my best friends in the world for the past 17 years (and counting) is black. I've heard him talk about things that he's endured and the way people have treated him growing up and even to this day, as we journey through our forties. It is truly sickening to me that people can act so ignorant to this day.

Racism is dumb any way you look at it. To think that you are better than someone else because of the color of their skin compared to yours is one of the most ludicrous mindsets one could have. Equality should mean equality. Racism is certainly not exclusive to blacks. Just this past season there were controversies surrounding Major League Baseball because of the lack of Latino coaches and managers. Look at the outcry against Muslims entering the country (again, seemingly instigated by the media) from Somalia and Syria.

I'm sure there are a ton of arguments headed my way for saying this, but in my opinion, if you want equality, it starts with disbanding organizations that are completely racially based, such as the NAACP. I agree with Stacey Dash when she says you can't have it both ways. But most of the time, that's the way it seems…that they want it both ways. They being the folks who want to generate a constant stream of reasons to complain. They want to claim they want equality while demanding to have businesses and award shows cater to minorities.

I'm not denying that racism exists, but I tend to believe that it is perpetuated by the media and those who seemingly go out of their way to play into every stereotype they can. If you don't want your teenager shot by police, teach them not to draw a weapon (even a fake one) on an officer. Teach your children that if they want to protest something, fine, but when you begin destroying property you're not doing yourselves any favors. What do you think of when you hear about vehicles being set on fire or businesses being looted "in protest"? When I hear it, I think thugs. And, unfortunately, even as a self-professed racially color-blind individual, I see a black man in my mind when I picture a thug. Why is that? Because that's who I see on the news perpetrating these actions during their "protests".

When the racial protests were going on in Ferguson, Missouri over police brutality, several buildings and vehicles were destroyed by fire set by the rioters. How exactly does that help? I mean, if it was war-time and you were lighting up enemy stockpiles to deplete their supplies, that's one thing. But to randomly set a business ablaze because you're unhappy with a court ruling and the police, doesn't make any sense. Honestly, what is that going to accomplish? I'll tell you. It makes you look like an uneducated moron. It makes you look like a thug. Same thing with shooting random police officers because you think there are too many police-involved deaths. It makes you look like a thug.

Please don't confuse my condemnation of the Ferguson riots as me being oblivious to racism or judging the African-American community for fighting back. I just think it was handled incorrectly. Trust me, I am all too aware that there are more white thugs in America than all of the other races combined. I only used Ferguson as an example because it's fresh in everyone's mind. One of the biggest promoters of racism, in my mind, is the mainstream media. Why does it have to be portrayed as a "hate crime" every time there is a fight between someone of color and a white person? Maybe they have a legitimate gripe with one another. Maybe one of them is truly a dick and finally got what he deserved. Just because a situation escalates to violence does not automatically mean that it was racially motivated.

I'm certainly not trying to imply that racism is one-sided. There are assholes all across the country. We're infested with bigots in every corner of civilization. From Donald Sterling to Dylann Roof, we see it everywhere we look. I just don't understand the premise. Take Sterling for example. He made millions and millions from owning an

NBA team that is comprised predominantly of black men. How do you look down on those who fill your pockets on a daily basis? I just can't comprehend that mentality. In Mississippi, in 2016, a couple was evicted because of their interracial marriage. You don't need me to recite all of the incidents that make headlines. Knowing that it is a learned behavior makes it even more disturbing, if you ask me. Who is teaching their children to hate like this? And why? What grudge do they have against another race that they think they need to breed this level of hate? It just doesn't make any sense.

On the other side of the fence, quit playing the race card every time you don't get what you want. I think that playing the race card breeds racism. The bigger the stink surrounding a "racial injustice" becomes, the more resentment it creates by those who didn't necessarily view it as such and/or don't have any real connection to the events in question. Does that sound insensitive? Be honest, how many of you look at the bigger picture every single time you hear something? The majority of the population looks at how something affects them personally, or their family directly. They don't stop to think about the ramifications of letting the behavior continue or of the snowball effect it will have on the very foundation of society (which I might add seems to be built on the sand from that vacation Bible school song).

I say we remove the title of minority, which by definition portrays being less than. Get rid of the term altogether. And along with the title, you have to throw out all of the stipulations and considerations that go along with being part of a minority. Equal means the same. The easiest way to spread a mentality of unity is to remove the divisions that are in place. Stop demanding anything because of your race or religion. If you want something, earn it. You truly do have the power to change your future. Earning your place in the world is hard work, but that doesn't mean someone should hand it to you. It means you have to buckle down and get it done if you want to attain your goals.

The real issue is the extremists from each racial sect and how they "protest" the issues. From Hispanic gang violence to KKK rallies to the riots in Baltimore or Ferguson, not a single one of these racially charged groups is going it about it properly. Quit being an asshole. It's that easy. If you're around people who are assholes, find new people to be around. Judge other people for yourself, don't listen to what someone else tells you. I imagine if I had been raised in the mid-1900's I would have at some point met my untimely demise for speaking my mind on these issues…but I guess I can't exactly rule it out without a shadow of a doubt even now.

Now that I've got you fired up, let's talk about sexism and LGBT rights. Who you want to sleep with or fantasize about is your business. It's between you and your partner(s). And, as long as it's consensual, who gives a shit? Or at least that should be the philosophy.

While I don't care what your sexual orientation is, the "I identify as…" thing has gotten out of hand. Facebook now offers over 50 options for gender identity when updating your profile. And in today's world where everyone gets everything they want, you have people who have decided they don't even "identify" as human. A 20-year-old Norwegian woman identifies as a cat and states she has known since she was 16 that she was a cat. A transgender man-turned-woman has decided that she is in fact a dragon and has had body modifying surgeries to remove her nose and ears in an effort to look more like the mythical reptile. A 52-year-old Canadian man left his wife and seven children because he feels he is a 6-year-old girl. While some of these options seem legit, many of these identities leave you feeling like it is someone's desperate attempt to become a unique snowflake. As I stated earlier, I don't care you who sleep with (or what) as long as it's all consensual. But things are heading to such an extreme that it's becoming laughable. As far as I know, there are still only about 4 variations on the human anatomy regarding sexual organs. You have a penis, you have a vagina, or have both or I suppose you could have neither. So how is it that we're up over 50 again?

Going hand in hand with this new identity crisis are the pronoun requests by those who believe themselves to be neither male or female. Someone may introduce themselves and state "My name is ____ and I identify as _____. My pronouns are ___, ____, and ___." For example, for myself, it could be said that I identify as male and my pronouns are he, him and his. But these days people go beyond the simply he or she and have even begun to create new pronouns adopted from other languages and try to incorporate them into the English vernacular. Some of these include "ze/hir/hirs," "ze/zir/zirs," and "xe/xem/xyr." There are yet others that want to be referred to as they/them/theirs.

There was a great scene in Season 7, Episode 4 of the Showtime series *Shameless* that illustrated this with great affect. One of the main characters, Ian Gallagher, is introduced to his partner's friends and the following dialogue occurs:

> [Friend #1] I'm... I'm Bethany. I'm a tri-racial cisgendered girl-fag. I identify as pansexual, and my pronoun is "she."
> [Ian] Okay.
> [Friend 2] Hi. Emerson. Gender-fluid heteroromantic demisexual mutt. And a redhead. My pronoun is "zie."
> [Friend 3] Hey. I'm Rabbit. Genderqueer tax attorney. I identify as Jennifer Aniston. Just kidding. Ve/vem/vir.
> [Friend 4] DX. Chinese Mexican agender intersex AFAB. My pronoun is "they."

[Ian] Okay. All right. Is it okay if I ask a few questions?

[Ian's partner] Better than to assume you know the answers.

[Ian] Um, what is inter... Uh, inter... intersex?

[Ian's partner] Ah, when a person is born with what is typically perceived as both male and female s*x organs.

[Ian] Oh, y... Uh, what, um... AFAB?

[Friend 4] Assigned Female At Birth... When your parents decide your gender without considering how you may identify in the future.

[Ian] Okay, and w-what's the whole, um, uh, pronoun thing?

[Ian's partner] When we talk about DX, we say, "Ask them if they would like a coffee."

[Ian] But there's only one of him. Her. Them. f*ck. I have no idea what I'm doing.

[Ian's partner] You'll get it.

What isn't captured above is what I can only describe as full-out contempt by Friend 4 when she has to explain AFAB and while Ian is stumbling over the pronoun labels.

This scene encompassed so much in a minute and a half of screen time, and posed the uneducated viewer so many questions that it had to be broken down. While doing some research on each of the terms I was unfamiliar with was enlightening to say the least, it also just seemed to prove what I've been saying all along. This is a group of individuals who are doing their damnedest to show themselves to be unique. Most have probably suffered unspeakable and inexcusable bias and bigotry throughout their lives just because of how they feel when it comes to choosing a partner. And I am in no way attempting to belittle them or take away from their right to enjoy their time with whomever they see fit. But there are many layers to this onion and it is my opinion that several of them need to be trimmed off and thrown away.

While I think everyone is entitled to be with the partner of their choosing, what the ever-living Hell is this nonsense? Searching for acceptance is one thing. Asking people to refer to you as a plural is something else entirely. Are you coexisting in your body with others? Are there multiple personalities in there that each demand their own say? I've seen *Split*, even the multiple personalities typically have names and genders. In my simple opinion, this goes back with the gender issue and it all boils down to two choices. There are still only two types of human sexual organs. And if you are a man who wants to be a woman, you can use your femininity and be a she. That's fine. But you are not a "they". You are not a plural. I guess if I start to hear people refer to themselves as "we" I should watch out for the rest of the Borg and get the Hell out of Dodge.

I am also always taken aback when I hear people who (wait, I guess that's not correct since not everyone identifies as a person these days) want to blame their parents because they chose a sex for them at birth. There are plenty of tirades across the web detailing how this is cruel and unjust to assign the term boy or girl to an infant.

While discussing how inclusive to be, it should also be pointed out that within the LGBT community there are discrepancies as well, so don't beat yourself up too much for not know all of the scenarios. Some websites use LGBT and others use LGBTQ. Yet others still now use what they feel to be even more inclusive acronyms such as LGBTQIA or LGBTQIAPD. The latter is comprised of Lesbian, Gay, Trans, Queer or Questioning, Intersex, Asexual, Pansexual and Demisexual.

Maybe I'm just an immature asshole for not buying into this whole line of thinking. I certainly don't view myself as homophobic. I have friends and family who are members of the LGBT community and I proudly support them and their rights. Maybe I'm too closed minded or maybe I'm simply jaded by my own mindset that not everyone requires a unique identifier. It reminds me of an elementary school "graduation" ceremony where every student is recognized and presented with a certificate in an effort to keep anyone from feeling left out. While awards for Perfect Attendance or Reading Excellence (for quantity of books read) are standard for these ceremonies, it gets a bit ridiculous when every single child in a grade of 110 children receives a certificate in some category. Those who failed to excel in any particular subject begin to receive awards for Best Sharer, Neatest

Desk or Best Giver of Compliments. Those are real, by the way. I found those last three on a teacher maintained website amongst a list of "fun awards for all students". But I digress...

These controversies regarding gender have escalated to the point of "bathroom laws" being passed in North Carolina. And while the debates may rage on regarding the difference between gender and sex, the mainstream media views them to be synonymous with each other for the purposes of these discussions. That North Carolina law, now infamously known as HB2, states that you have to use the restroom of the gender that is listed on your birth certificate. The LGBT community is outraged. Businesses from Disney to the NBA to the NCAA have declared they won't introduce any new business or events in the state unless the laws are changed. Musical artists have cancelled stops on their tours. The whole thing could be resolved by simply making all of the public restrooms unisex. Many larger metropolitan areas already have enacted laws to make all single occupancy bathrooms unisex.

Hell the idea of unisex bathrooms has been around since at least the early 2000's when they appeared on the television show *Ally McBeal*. Why can't people be adult enough to make common sense decisions? There have been non-discrimination ordinances (NDO) in place around the world for over 35 years now. In that time, there has only been one documented case of sexual assault in a place where an NDO existed, and that was in Canada back in 2012 in a women's shelter. So none of these fears that the state of North Carolina wanted you to believe are true. Thankfully, in 2017, HB2 was repealed after being on the books for a year. I would guess the loss of tourist cash flow from sports tournaments and concerts probably helped some of the lawmakers snap back to their senses. But, I assure you, no one goes to a public restroom unless they have business to conduct at the toilet or sink. Have you been in one lately? They're disgusting. I would wager that 99% of the people you see in the bathroom are there for the same reason you are. When they close the stall door and sit down, what difference does it make to you what they have between their legs?

Unfortunately, North Carolina isn't the state to create laws specifically aimed at the LGBT community. According to the HRC, a Washington-based group called the Human Rights Campaign, 252 bills were introduced in 2016 with eight of them passing to become law. As of May 2017, an additional 131 have been introduced nationwide, 24 of which are in Texas alone. Congressmen and women who support the bills state they are protecting their constituents' religious freedoms. But are you really protecting someone's beliefs properly if you are infringing on someone else's? I can't imagine being a business owner and turning down business because I didn't like who someone wanted to marry, it just doesn't make sense. Are they asking you to host the wedding in your store? Sure, turn that down if you're not equipped for it or don't want to do it, but refusing to bake them a cake just because they want to put two grooms on top? Grow the fuck up! It is a widely published statistic that fifty percent of all small businesses fail within their first five years. When you hear stories about refusing customers due to sexual orientation, it surprises me that the percentage isn't even greater. There are some things that you don't have to have a business degree to know, or at least you should, and accepting every customer should be one of those "no-brainer" concepts.

In 2017, there are multiple universities that offer training and information regarding what is being called "heterosexual privilege". Marshall University in Huntington, WV is the first University to train its staff on the understanding of "heterosexual privilege". The University of Calgary's "Campaign for Positive Space" webpage defines "heterosexual privilege" as follows:

> Webster's dictionary defines "privilege" as the right or immunity granted as an advantage or favor to some but not to others. Heterosexual privilege confers unearned and unchallenged advantages and rewards on heterosexuals solely as a result of their sexual orientation.

That same website goes on to list sixteen things that they believe represent "heterosexual privilege", while Carleton College in Minnesota lists twenty-one. These range from "When I am told about our national heritage or about "civilization", I am shown that people of my sexual orientation made it what it is" and "I can turn on the television or open to the front page of the paper and see people of my sexuality widely represented" to "Assuming that all people and relationships are heterosexual, unless otherwise known." Now, I'm not a historian, a statistician, a scientist, teacher or a marketing genius, but is it not common sense to cater to the majority in most cases? According to a CDC study published in the Washington Post, and corroborated with multiple topical internet searches, only 3.3 % of Americans adults identify as gay or other, with another 1.3 % identifying as bisexual. So just given the law of averages, would it not make sense that the bulk of historical accounts involve heterosexuals? That the majority of television programming and movie content will be heterosexual because the majority of the writers, actors, networks, etc. are heterosexual. This is not a malicious attempt to stomp out the LGBT community. This falls into some of the same nauseating whiny attitudes that I discussed earlier with the #OscarsSoWhite fiasco. Should the mentioning of LGBT be included in history lessons? I think the answer to that question lies with another query. Is it relevant to the story or events that are being documented?

In interviews regarding proposed health care laws, a doctor was quoted as stating "…most of the people who have C-sections identify as women…" and then later in the same interview, "A majority of people who get pregnant identify as women…" What the Hell else would they identify as? I don't know of any male pregnancies, or the world would put them on display. This is part of what I can't comprehend about the whole gender identity discussion. You can't have your cake and eat it too. Even those who are transgender will tell you they are either male or female, and very adamantly in some cases. What you prefer sexually shouldn't have anything to do with your gender. So exactly what else do anatomically female humans who have babies identify as? Inquiring minds want to know.

As I've stated multiple times already, I don't care who you want to be with as long as it's consensual. And shouldn't that be the general philosphy held by everyone? Isn't that what the LGBT community is ultimately striving for? If that's the case, why are they offended by seeing too much heterosexuality in print and on screen? Because everyone feels like they are a special unicorn that needs to be catered to. We've stopped listening to common sense and now have to fall at the alter of political correctness or be considered a racist bigot or to be in support of a radical organization like the

Klu Klux Klan or Neo-Nazis. It couldn't possibly be that we just didn't give a shit about their cause and that's why we didn't promote or highlight it. And when I say I don't give a shit about their cause, I don't mean that I don't care about the rights of the individuals. But what is being asked for more often than not, in recent years, is not a right. They're asking for special considerations while holding a sign that says equal rights. And if I'm going to give them the equal rights they are begging for, then I am not going to go out of my way to demand things in the name of their causes. Don't tell me to treat you equal and then demand I give you preference over someone else just because you are a member of the LGBT community. I assure you, no one gives me anything based on my sexual orientation, race or gender. But, what do I know, I'm completely saddled with "male prvilege", "white privilege" and "heterosexual privilege". I wonder if there is an overweight privilege I can tap in to?

In Lexington, KY in early 2017 a new public high school was preparing to open. The school was being built on part of what used to be a renowned horse farm known for producing fine stallions. So in an homage to the heritage of the land, the school planned to use Stallions as their mascot. But immediately after announcing to the public their plans, the school board was met with an outcry from people stating that the mascot choice was not gender neutral and demanding it be changed.

Within days of making the announcement, the county responded by stating the mascot name would be changed and voted on by students in the district. For the record, at the time of this writing, there are at least 10 other schools that use Stallions as their mascot, including two universities. While I agree, stallion equals male, who honestly gets offended by this? The petition that started the outcry labeled it as "inappropriate and sexist" but is that really true? While the petition on change.org didn't reach its goal of 500 signatures, it did gain national attention by the media. Where are the controversies surrounding every school that has a ram for their mascot? The definition is the same as for a stallion. An uncastrated male ____. Yet over a dozen colleges and universities use a ram as their mascot, not to mention the hundreds of high schools across the country.

And this is the problem. Something doesn't have to be truly offensive for it to gain traction these days. The simple whisper of a controversy is enough to make corporations, schools and organizations bow to unsubstantiated threats. And there is always someone out there trying to find a way to be offended by what you do. I'm convinced that some have no other purpose in life than to twist things out of context in a purposeful attempt to wreak negativity upon the world.

Celebrities are a frequent target in perceived scandals regarding racism and sexism. During an interview surrounding the release of *Captain America: Civil War*, Chris Evans and Jeremy Renner were interviewed about their thoughts on Scarlett Johansson's *Black Widow* character and her interest in *Bruce Banner*. Renner responded by saying "she's a slut" and everyone in the interview laughed and continued. But the internet was outraged. So much so, that Renner was forced to issue an apology, "I am sorry that this tasteless joke about a fictional character offended anyone. It was not meant to be serious in any way. Just poking fun during an exhausting and tedious press tour." Google it if you feel intrigued. The comment was clearly meant as a joke. Why would anyone feel the need to make it more than that?

After the death of Carrie Fisher, fellow thespian Steve Martin posted what he intended to be a tribute on his Twitter feed. "When I was a young man, Carrie Fisher she was the most beautiful creature I had ever seen. She turned out to be witty and bright as well." The backlash was immediate and ultimately resulted in him taking down the post. Some said his tweet focused on her looks instead of her talents or impact. I read it as if he found her to be more than just a pretty face. But the internet is a fickle bitch.

Fisher, herself a renowned feminist, found some of the media generated frenzies to be ridiculous. In 2015, a man from Pennsylvania gained national attention for claiming he was offended by an action figure depicting *Princess Leia* as *Jabba the Hutt*'s prisoner. You know, the "Slave Leia" gold bikini outfit that is one of the most iconic costumes ever worn on screen. Fred Hill was quoted as saying "I got 2 daughters I don't need seeing that crap… They're like dad why does this doll have a chain around its neck. I don't have any answers. I was just blown away looking at it." When asked about the incident and the attempts to gain public outrage, Fisher was quoted in the *Wall Street Journal* as responding as follows:

> WSJ: There's been some debate recently about whether there should be no more merchandise with you in the "Return of the Jedi" bikini.
>
> Fisher: I think that's stupid.
>
> WSJ: To stop making the merchandise?
>
> Fisher: The father who flipped out about it, "What am I going to tell my kid about why she's in that outfit?" Tell them that a giant slug captured me and forced me to wear that stupid outfit, and then I killed him because I didn't like it. And then I took it off. Backstage.

Then to the *L.A. Times* she responded in similar fashion saying, "How about telling his daughter that the character is wearing that outfit not because she's chosen to wear it. She's been forced to wear it. She's a prisoner of a giant testicle who has a lot of saliva going on and she does not want to wear that thing and it's ultimately that chain, which you're now indicating is some sort of accessory to S&M, that is used to kill the giant saliva testicle…. That's asinine." Rest in peace, Carrie. Rest in peace.

Sometimes, people get offended these days for no particular reason at all. I pick on the Millennials a lot, but it seems to be repeatedly justified when I do my research.

As an example, take the Father-Daughter dances that have grown in popularity over the past few years. These are held at elementary schools across the country, particularly around Valentine's Day as a way for fathers to have a night with their daughters and give them a special date night experience. Typically both will dress formally and have a sit-down dinner preceding the dance. It's not limited to just schools hosting these events, and in some cases they are held in a civic center or other ballroom setting. Mother-Son dances are held in some places, although they are less common. I bring these up because, like everything else these days, they have become a source of controversy.

In Rhode Island, a single mother filed a complaint with the ACLU because her daughter wasn't allowed to attend their Father-Daughter dance. They deemed it an injustice and took the school district to court. It was determined that while federal gender discrimination laws exempt such events, Rhode Island's does not. So in this case you have an instance where someone is simply jealous of something another is doing. I don't know why the woman is single, and I don't care. Based on what I know of her from this one story, maybe it's because she's a pretentious bitch. But regardless, why do today's people think they have the right to ruin everyone else's fun just because they don't qualify for something? Does misery love company that much? Really?

I would have never dreamed of complaining about something like this. If I don't meet the prerequisites for something, I shrug it off and think "oh well." But that's not the way this generation's mind works. To them it's ok to put everyone else out, just so that they feel satisfied. I compare it to elementary schools who make kids who bring peanut butter products in their lunches, sit at a separate table because one child in the school has an allergy and they didn't want them to feel singled out by segregating them from the others. So hundreds of children have to watch what they bring and be isolated from the group if they want to enjoy a peanut butter and jelly sandwich, all because one parent isn't able to properly teach their child how to deal with their allergy and avoid exposure.

You'd think that this would be the only complaint (or type of complaint) regarding these dances, but you'd be wrong. A Millennial mother over on a website called www.romper.com also thinks that Father-Daughter dances should be ended. She believes, and I quote "These aren't sweet. They aren't cute. They're creepy, and they seek to enforce patriarchal notions of femininity." She rambles on a feminist rant, citing incest and rape statistics and how this is bordering on a "Lolita-type fetish." A little deeper in the article she mentions "I don't have daughters — only sons. But these attitudes harm them, too. It primes my sons to grow up to expect girls who are submissive and passive — not equal partners. These ideas force them into the gendered notions of the patriarchy, where men make the choices and women obey. It's only a sidestep from rape culture, and it's my job, first and foremost, to bring my sons up not to rape."

What the hell happened to this woman when she was younger? From reading this article, I have determined that she is a single-mother who either didn't know her father, was abused by him, didn't like him or was raised by a lesbian couple. Now, in all fairness, this website when you search it on Google comes up as "A parenting site by millennial women for millennial women. Let's all grow up together." and scrolling through the articles the appear at the bottom of this one I found as many headlines for Jessa Duggar, George Clooney, as well as ABC's *Scandal*, *How To Get Away With Murder*, and *Grey's Anatomy* as there were about actual parenting, so take its credibility for what it's worth. But the point falls in line with the ACLU complaint in my opinion. Somebody wanted to do something and couldn't and now they want everyone else to turn against it like they have.

I saw a great quote on the gender wage gap that said "Want to close wage gap? Step one: Change your major from feminist dance therapy to electrical engineering." A Harvard professor extensively studied the wage gap and has determined that it is not based on gender as much as it is priorities. As their careers progress, women tend to look for flexibility in their jobs to allow them to balance work and home life. It is a higher priority to them than it is of men of the same age, experience and skill level. The study went on to illustrate that men at that same point in life tend to work harder and put in more hours. Obviously, that's not always the case. Ask the CEO of Pepsi, IBM, Hewlett Packard Enterprise, Oracle or Xerox. Oh, they're all women, by the way. As with racism, I understand that gender inequality is a real thing in our culture today. But you don't have to let yourself be a victim of it. Change the perception. Take control of your future and stop sitting on the couch saying "I can't because I'm just a ___..."

Obviously I'm not going to touch on every facet of racism or sexism here in this book. It's not what the book is about. I just wanted to highlight a handful of ridiculously extreme cases to add some spice to the story. Agree with me or disagree, it really doesn't matter. This is the nation we live in. This is what we've become. A collective of oversensitive prudes who want to present as if everything should be about them and their precious feelings and opinions.

"The day the child realizes that all adults are imperfect, he becomes an adolescent; the day he forgives them, he becomes an adult; the day he forgives himself, he becomes wise."

- Canadian journalist, author, poet, playwright and Governor General's Award winner, Alden Nowlan

Kids Can't Be Kids

I talked about how childhood differs for today's youth compared to those of us over the age of 35 in my last book, but thanks to a handful of inspired readers sharing their stories and findings, along with the vastness of the internet and ever-growing ridiculousness of our society, it would appear that there is plenty of fresh content for me to pass along.

One topic that is almost always sure to start a controversy, almost as much as religion and politics, is parenting. Everyone who has a child believes they know how it should be raised, and actually, quite a few who don't will not hesitate to share their opinions on the matter to anyone who will listen. The one consistency within the topic of parenting is that everyone has a different viewpoint.

While there is not any single defined guideline for raising a child in a proven method, one thing you can be sure of is that we've grown soft over the years. The days of being spanked in school and cutting a switch for your father to whip you with are shades of the past. If a man removed his belt to whip a child in today's society, he would be charged with child abuse and possible jail time. Just ask Adrian Peterson of the Minnesota Vikings. He was indicted on a felony charge for reckless or negligent injury to a child in 2014 and missed the entire season on suspension from the NFL, all because he whipped his son with a switch. The boy was taken to a doctor's visit by his mother, and the doctor's office called authorities to report abuse. Everyone under the age of 30 screamed in outrage of these heinous acts of abuse and how the man should have served jail time for his actions.

Peterson explained that this was the way he was raised and he hadn't done anything he wasn't subjected to himself as a child. Does that make it abuse? No. It means he came from an upbringing where discipline was recognized and rules were followed to avoid the consequences of disobeying them.

But today's is a society filled with time outs and acceptance. Children are no longer punished physically for their wrongdoing, the new preferred methods involve psychological punishments which are widely considered less intrusive. One of the so called benefits of using a time out is "the parent-child relationship quickly returns to normal following the use of time-out." Do you want to know why that is? Because it doesn't work...or at least not as well as a millennial parenting website would like you to believe. Studies have shown that anyone attempting to use time out as a punishment still by the time the child is age 6, is more than likely just affording the child an uninterrupted chance to plot their revenge for whatever they deem to be the injustice. Other studies delve farther into the psychological ramifications of the time out periods and have found that it can send the wrong message to a child entirely to place them in time out. Because of the basic human need for acceptance and socialization, a time out can present to a child that if they mess up they will be ostracized by their peers and loved ones. Those feelings can quickly turn to the belief that they will only be accepted if they have everything in their life together, and that if they are imperfect, they will be doomed to be alone.

The main selling point of a time out is that it is supposed to be a non-violent, less physical form of punishment. An alternative to screaming at or spanking a child. Hell, from the time out enforcements that I've witnessed over the years, there is usually a more physical altercation than if the parent would have simply spanked them. The child kicking and screaming and the parent grabbing them by an arm and dragging them to the corner, chair, couch, their room or wherever the time out was supposed to take place.

Is there a fine line between a spanking (or whipping) and abuse? Sure. But the vast majority of parents who employ spanking as punishment know where that line is instinctually and how to avoid crossing it. I can attest that I grew up being spanked. If you got in trouble in school, you got sent to the principal's office for a spanking. When you got home, you got another one from your parents. If you stayed out past when you were supposed to, you got spanked. If you picked on your sibling, you got spanked. Most anything you did that warranted punishment at all, resulted in a spanking. The spanking could come in the form of a hand, a paddle, a belt or a switch. Teachers had their paddles hanging on their classroom walls like trophies. Some teachers would swat at hands with rulers. I even had one teacher who would throw a metal bell across the classroom when she was upset.

Now, I'm sure when I was still in my pre-teen years, I probably felt like I was being abused because I was whipped as often as I was. I mean, it's not like I was ever given a spanking or paddling that was unwarranted, I was a boy and into everything. All of my punishments were just and deserved. If I did something wrong, there were consequences which taught me not to repeat that action again in the future. As such, since achieving adulthood, I cannot ever remember having a thought of abuse throughout my childhood. I have never reflected on my upbringing and felt like I was a victim or that my parents should have been charged or jailed for the way they raised us.

Unfortunately, it would appear that mine is no longer thought of as conventional wisdom. The twenty-somethings and thirty-somethings of the world today all feel like they have been slighted by their parents or pigeon-holed by society. Everything that occurs is a travesty and they have a burning desire to share it with the world in an effort for their plight to go viral or have someone justify their feelings.

In Maryland, an 8th-grader was charged as a juvenile with second-degree assault before being released to his mother, after kissing a 14 year old girl on the mouth. When did it become a crime for a 13 year old to kiss a 14 year old? This wasn't a sexual assault. There was no malicious intent to rape or escalate. It was a boy kissing a girl on a dare at school one day. I discussed it in my last book, but I just don't understand a school's inability to use common sense. While I understand not wanting a harassing environment for any student, there is a difference between unwanted sexual advances and a kiss.

But, this is one area that society is surprisingly gender neutral. In Florida, a 12-year-old girl was brought up on misdemeanor battery charges because she pinched a boy's butt at school. Again, the school over reacted, in my opinion, and suspended the girl. But what made this one worse was it was the boy's mother who contacted the police after she learned what happened. The only way the charges could be dropped was if the girl underwent drug testing and performed community service. What the ever-living Hell kind of crazy is this woman? I get looking after your children, but again, we're talking about middle school kids. This wasn't a boss grabbing his secretary or even a teacher copping a feel on a student. This was two middle school kids being middle school kids.

Remember a couple of paragraphs ago when I was making fun of people having grudges against their parents? In Illinois, twenty-something siblings Steven and Kathryn Miner, sued their mother, Kimberly Garrity, for bad parenting during their childhood years. Their claims included, their mother not sending her son college care packages, not buying her daughter the homecoming dress she wanted, and that their birthday cards never included cash or checks, just the printed Hallmark sentiments. Thankfully, the $500,000 lawsuit was dismissed in a court of appeals. The judge stated

"Such alleged actions are unpleasant and perhaps insensitive, and some would arguably fall outside the realm of 'good mothering,' but they are not so shocking as to form a basis for a claim for intentional infliction of emotional distress," adding that ruling in favor of the children "could potentially open the floodgates to subject family child rearing to ... excessive judicial scrutiny and interference."

Worse than that, in New York, a thirteen year old boy filed a "Wrongful Life" lawsuit against his parents because he was born with red hair. The boy claims that his parents knew their children would very likely inherit their red hair and they have caused him a "voluntary prejudice" by having him, knowing he would be born into a life of pain and suffering. He demanded $1.35 million for pain and suffering and another $800,000 for "loss of enjoyment of life". There have been other "Wrongful Life" lawsuits over the past few years, but this is the first to be based around a physical trait. The boy cites that he is continually ridiculed and told he doesn't have a soul, as well as being labeled with a variety of red haired nicknames such as Carrot Top, Strawberry Shortcake and others. I've been called Fat Ass by a passing car when I was on a golf green. Where's my "Wrongful Life" suit? Oh yeah, I'm not a pussy, so I didn't file one.

The youth of today will never have an opportunity to learn the same things we did when we were their age, because society won't let us teach them the same. When we were kids we played outside until it got dark, and on the weekends, that meant putting in 14-16 hours out there. We climbed trees, rode our bikes and skateboards without helmets and pads, shot bottle rockets out of pop bottles and melted models with a lighter we lifted from our parents. We were dropped off at the field for practice and games, or walked there on our own and it was a treat if your parents came to watch, and no one stayed to watch practices.

Today, kids aren't allowed out of the yard without supervision. If they were forced to go outside and spend the day, the neighbors would probably call the authorities and accuse you of neglect. Helmets are required for anything involving wheels, and if you are going on a skateboard, scooter or skates, you have to have knee and elbow pads as well.

Cities ban sledding during the winter because they believe there are too many injuries and they are so paranoid of the "sue for anything" crowd that is likely to sue the city for an accident incurred while sleigh riding in a city park. It wouldn't matter that the parents were present and most likely the ones who suggested the location and chose the equipment. All that would matter was that it couldn't possibly be their fault if their children were injured.

Sports practices are carefully monitored under

the watchful eye of every parent who has a child on the team. They are all judging the instruction the children are being given, never volunteering themselves, but ridiculing the coach's every move and all the while remaining vigilant of pedophiles and kidnappers that the Lifetime channel has taught them are lurking around every corner.

The helicopter parents, you know the ones who hover around every single activity and interaction their children have, feel they are entitled to something, regardless of if they have put in the work to earn it or not. That their children are entitled to something just for being there. But sadly, these helicopter parents are no longer the biggest issue. Now there are "lawnmower parents". These parents go through in front of their children to make sure there are no obstacles in the path of precious little Johnny or Suzi. Parents will complete applications and forms for their children, even college aged students. They'll then follow up and contact teachers and professors on behalf of their child in an effort to sort out grades or ask forgiveness for assignment miscues.

Ironically, it is the children who end up bearing the brunt of this behavior. While the lawnmower parent is out attempting to clear a path for their little darling, they are in actuality creating a sense of dependency for their children that could cause a lack of personal motivation, the inability to make a decision without guidance from others, and a sense of lowered self-esteem, wrongly believing that they aren't good enough to do things by themselves and that they can't be trusted to complete tasks on their own. It can create a situation where the child is unprepared to deal with life's obstacles. Unable to navigate a path alone, and poorly equipped to deal with confrontations, small or large. From fellow students to coworkers, to professors, teachers and superiors, the ability to sort through a situation and find the resolution by themselves has been taken away by the lawnmower parent.

I know every generation feels like they can't believe how much the times have changed when it comes to raising their kids, but when compared to our parents and grandparents (aside from technological advances), it would appear that the last thirty years have drastically went downhill in regards to how children are treated and/or expected to behave.

Everyone is always looking for a label or an excuse for every action and behavior pattern. Children are deemed to have attention deficit disorder (ADD) or attention deficit hyperactivity disorder (ADHD) if they fidget in school. This was a condition that has been discussed and documented dating all the way back to the 1700s, but it wasn't until the late 1990s that it gained prominence in modern society and the "documented" cases skyrocketed.

I am not saying that it doesn't exist, I am not a

scientist or expert in a medical field of study. It just seems to be a convenient catch-all for parents, teachers, and doctors to place blame on a condition for the child's behavior rather than accept responsibility for it. The entire time my sister and I attended school, I know of one boy who was diagnosed with ADHD and took a daily dose of Ritalin. From my experience with my own child, any time a kid talks in an elementary classroom now the teacher pushes for the parents to have them tested for ADHD.

What happened to teachers being able to control their students? Multiple answers all converge to paint that picture. The removal of corporal punishment in schools led to an increase in detention, suspensions and expulsions. Parents complained that pick-up arrangements couldn't be modified and bus schedules needed to be maintained to the point that after school detention became obsolete. Same thing for detention prior to the school day. Detention moved to the lunch hour, but they still had to allow for the kids to eat, so it was shortened to the point that it is ineffective. With all of these barbless punishments, kids realized they could get away with more in class because nothing would come of it in the end. Teachers who raise their voices are attacked by social media and parents demanding punishments to be handed down by the schools or school boards. Parents won't allow anyone else to administer discipline to their precious snowflakes, so even the school officials become handicapped to prevent undesirable behavior.

When you couple all of that with the notion of everybody is a winner and no one gets left behind, you end up with teachers catering to the slowest students, rather than finding a midpoint to focus their attention. When we were young, students were placed in their classrooms by their grades and test results. The practice was known as ability grouping and it allowed the teachers to move at a comfortable speed for all students, without leaving anyone behind or causing excessive boredom in accelerated students. In elementary school we had 1st through 4th group. At the conclusion of a school year, for example, 1st group may end a text book on chapter 16 while 4th group ended on chapter 10. What eventually happened was in the nineties, parents began to become upset with the group their precious unicorns were placed in complained that it was discrimination to segregate the children based on test scores. Opponents argued that it placed a label on a child that followed them throughout their school years and that it tended to funnel minorities a place in which they would receive a lower level of education. Honestly I don't see how that could be the case. If the groupings were based on test results, they would be funneled by their intelligence rather than race or social status.

As an adult, I couldn't tell you which of my

classmates were in which groupings as we were growing up. I could probably name the majority of my group (roughly 26-28 kids), just because I spent more time with them through elementary school, and I could probably name the majority of the kids in my graduating class of 110. But I couldn't tell you what group the other seventy or so participated in when we were young. While the groupings could have given some indicators of intelligence, it didn't mean that being in 3rd group meant you weren't as smart as those in 1st group. It simply meant that you learned at a different pace than some of your peers.

Is it a coincidence that the National Education Association did away with ability grouping in the late nineties? The same time when ADHD cases began to spike across the country? I think it was less coincidence and more cause and effect. Once teachers were forced to move at the pace of their slowest students, the more advanced children became bored. Boredom in a child breeds activity. Talking in class; becoming the class clown; tapping toes, pencils, fingers, etc.; day dreaming; pestering their classmates. All of these are indicators of boredom. It doesn't mean that the children all have ADHD. But, with an ADHD diagnosis comes medication. With medication comes docile children. Docile children sit quietly and don't disrupt classrooms with their behavior.

As if all of these factors aren't enough to show what has happened to our youth, now add in the mentality that everyone is a winner. Everyone deserves to move on. Some schools across the country have a policy in which no one fails. Everyone gets at least a C grade and moves on, regardless of the grades they should have earned. Standardized tests became the driving force for budgetary allocations and therefore became the focus of a school's attention rather than a mandatory function they performed at the end of the school year. Those test scores literally mean jobs to teachers and as a result the focus, for months at a time, leading up to the standardized tests becomes testing content and procedures. Regular class itineraries are aborted in favor of agendas which put a child in a better position to score well on the standard tests. All of this focus on a single test result can also induce boredom from even a moderate student.

In my non-expert-in-any-field opinion, the culmination of all of the above changes have led us to the increased number of ADHD cases documented each year. Parents fail to discipline children at home properly and send them to school for instruction. Schools are wary of lawsuits and complaints and attempting to appease every demographic and wind up having more lenient standards and rules. The leniency gets taken in excess by the students who know they cannot be punished in any method that has teeth. Therefore they act out, they disrupt, and they do what they want while on school property with no repercussions. Teachers couldn't possibly accept blame for not engaging the children and complain to parents that their kids aren't paying attention. Parents won't accept responsibility for their child's actions and take them to the doctor seeking a condition that could result in these undesirable behaviors. Doctors then pull out their catch-all diagnosis and "wallah!" A condition has been found that matches the child's symptoms and medication is prescribed that will calm the student's nerves. No one could fathom the idea that the child wasn't receiving the attention they needed at home and turned to their school classroom as an outlet for their frustrations. It couldn't be that mommy is a single mother of two children by two different fathers and is so wrapped up in trying to find a husband that she ignores the kids at home. The children over eat because the only time they get attention is when they say they're hungry. When they go to school they feel as though they've been held captive to their own imaginations and seek approval and attention from anyone that will listen or entertain their actions. When the child gets in trouble at school, a medical condition is the only acceptable possibility that the mother can believe, because they are the perfect parent and there couldn't be anything wrong or missing at home that could cause their adorable little unicorn to behave in such a manner.

If you don't like the idea of just taking my

opinions on the matter, a family psychologist (Dr. John Rosemond) and pediatrician (Dr. Bose Ravenel) collaborated to publish an entire book on the subject titled *"The Diseasing of America's Children: Exposing the ADHD Fiasco and Empowering Parents to Take Back Control"* In it, they discuss how parents, teachers and even professionals are deceived along with the short and long-term dangers of behavioral drugs when used with children. They specifically call out the education system and discuss how schools are unwittingly perpetuating this societal mindset.

Personally, I believe there is no small correlation between the wussification of our youth and the increase in single parents. In 1960, the percentage of children being raised in a single parent home was 9 percent. In 1980, it was closer to nineteen. In recent years the percentage has ballooned to over 34 percent. Is there a direct line that can be drawn between the number of kids from single parent homes and some of the changes that have taken root in our society? Absolutely.

Single parents tend to come with a preset disposition that puts them on the defensive regarding even the slightest detail of their parenting expertise. While most people would tell you that they don't know everything there is to know about raising a child, you'll get less modesty and more snarkiness when posing the same question to a single parent. Now, I'm not a religious fanatic that believes that you have to have a "traditional family" of a husband and wife. But I do think that raising a child requires cooperation of at least two individuals working toward the child's best interest. It doesn't have to be in marriage. It doesn't have to be of opposite sexes. But it requires help. There is a reason the old adage "it takes a village…" is still used today.

But this is not what today's single parent wants to hear. They believe they can do it all. They can be the father figure, the mother figure, the role model, the disciplinarian, the chauffer, the cook, the maid all while maintaining an active social life. No one dare tell them that they need boundaries for their little darlings. How could someone who has already raised their own successful children presume to offer advice or tutelage to them? They are strong an independent. They do not need a man or a partner in their life to raise a well-behaved child. Their child gets everything they need from them and them alone. It is not necessary to inundate them with proven techniques or instruction because they know what they are doing and they love their children. How could you question their parenting skills?

Now I geared that last section toward a single mother, and that isn't to say there aren't plenty of single fathers out there. But studies show that approximately 81 percent of single parents are single mothers. Of those, almost 34 percent have never been married. So, I am not saying that single fathers don't have the same attitudes or problems, I am simply following the statistics with my examples.

This "I can do it all" attitude from these single parents many times relies on the child being the sole point of focus for their attention. This leads to helicopter and lawnmower parenting in every aspect of the child's life. Unfortunately, the overprotection can lead to severe consequences in the child's social development. Sometimes no one even sees it when it occurs. A child who has been raised as the center of attention, without any obstacles in their life, without any discomforts from life's trials and tribulations can reach college age without every experiencing a social conflict. If everything is easy for the entirety of their childhood, they will never learn how to cope with disappointment or loss. This can lead to students who drop out of college when their grades take a nosedive. Young adults who get divorced the first time they have an argument with their spouse. Employees who quit their jobs the first time they have a boss who expects a certain level of performance from them.

Childhood isn't supposed to be easy. Sure, I hope that most people are able to reflect on their childhood with fond memories, but not everything is roses and puppy dogs. Children need to be able to fail. They need to be able to struggle at times. Through these experiences, they will develop the life skills they need to function as an adult.

And we'll get to that more in the next chapter…

"I used to play sports. Then I realized you can buy trophies. Now I am good at everything."

- former writer for The Daily Show and Late Night with Conan O'Brien, stand-up comedian and actor, Demetri Martin

Sports

I know the majority of my first book discussed sports at the youth level, but those aren't the only problems I see with the sports world in general. Many of the topics I discussed in *8th Place Ribbon* have gained national attention in the past couple of years.

One of the most discussed topics is that of participation trophies. In August 2015, Pittsburgh Steelers linebacker, James Harrison gained the national spotlight when he posted on his social media account that he was sending back the participation trophies his sons received. He was quoted as stating:

> "I came home to find out that my boys received two trophies for nothing, participation trophies! While I am very proud of my boys for everything they do and will encourage them till the day I die, these trophies will be given back until they EARN a real trophy. I'm sorry I'm not sorry for believing that everything in life should be earned and I'm not about to raise two boys to be men by making them believe that they are entitled to something just because they tried their best...cause sometimes your best is not enough, and that should drive you to want to do better...not cry and whine until somebody gives you something to shut u up and keep you happy."

After writing a book that focused on this very topic, I for one whole-heartedly agree with this concept. My son has participation trophies in the house, but he could do whatever he likes with them. About the time he became a teenager he got rid of all the baseball, soccer and basketball trophies and informed us it was because not only did he not care about those sports any longer, he also knew he didn't do anything to earn them. His baseball team was good, but there were no championships for minor league, so the trophies still held no value or meaning to him. Soccer and basketball were just things he tried when he was younger. He did keep all of his football trophies, as he is still passionate about the game and while he only has a couple that were earned, he still values his experiences on the field and with his teams. I don't have a problem with that philosophy.

Just a little later on in 2015, Kia ran an ad campaign that prominently featured a father upset that his son was given a participation trophy from his youth football team. In the commercial, the dad brings up that they beat all the other teams and that everyone received the same trophy and in the end he pulls the nameplate that reads "Participation" off of the trophy and takes a marker and writes "Champs" on the base before handing it back to his son.

Thankfully, the idea of earning trophies or medals and doing away with participation trophies seems to be catching on. College coaches have voiced their concerns. They are the front line at witnessing the travesty that has befallen our youth. Mike Leach, head coach of the football team at Washington State University has said, "It's not whether you win or lose, it's the team that has the most fun. All the crap like that. All the stuff that's contaminated America where they give everyone a trophy and don't keep score in little league anymore" when asked about what's wrong. University of Louisville women's basketball coach Jeff Walz discussed the matter in a press conference after losing a couple of games in a row. He specifically cited the "everyone gets a trophy" mentality as a problem and discussed how it is the generation that is reaching college now that has been taught that they are all winners and lack the ability and drive to better themselves the way a team needs to in an effort to compete.

HBO's *Real Sports* did an entire episode titled "Trophy Culture" which focused entirely on participation trophies and the ramifications of receiving them. In their research, they found college professors, teachers, doctors and researchers who all drew a direct line from the trophy mentality to the issues that these kid are dealing with after they start entering colleges and the workforce. All of them shared the same basic premise, which was that it breeds an entitlement mentality. C. Robert Cloninger, a doctor at Washington University in St. Louis, told HBO that there are biological ramifications realized as a result of this culture, referred to as partial-reinforcement extinction effect. "All that means is that if you constantly reward a kid, you spoil them, and you don't build a capacity for them to be resilient to frustration." Cloninger goes on to add, "We have to get over the notion that everyone has to be a winner in the United States. It just isn't true."

In some instances, the leagues have begun attempting to prevent this atmosphere and to place an emphasis on performance instead of participation. Some leagues have issued statements that they will no longer be purchasing participation trophies and will only reward the top performers. In one instance, a soccer league in Los Angeles did away with participation trophies for anyone over the age of eight only to have the parents follow behind and buy them anyway. One of the most concerning details about this was that the "kids" whose parents bought trophies were 19 years old. Nineteen! On one hand this demonstrates the extreme problems with conditioning kids to expect a reward, and on the other I wonder if the same thing would have happened if it had taken place in another sport. I have always held a low opinion for the game of soccer, and stories like this just feed into every stereotype and bad depiction I've ever encountered.

But it doesn't stop with youth. The Indianapolis Colts hung a banner that says "2014 AFC Finalist" after losing the AFC Championship game to the Patriots. On the surface you may ask what is wrong with that? The standard for a season where a team loses in the playoffs is to make a sign that reads "AFC South Champion" or "2014 AFC South Division Champions". The Colts aren't the only ones who try to fluff their resume. There are tournaments and leagues where a celebration is held and a presentation is given to a team for finishing second out of three teams. The underlying issue here is the same as it is someone trying to portray something more than what occurred. And that feeds directly into the youth perspective in sometimes dramatic fashion. Some individual sports that do not give participation trophies have adopted practices where they will name one child as "most improved" and another as "most coachable", etc. They continue creating titles and categories until everyone on the team gets an award for some kind. Then they claim they don't hand out participation trophies.

As soon as children realize that they do not have to work hard in practice or even win games, that they'll get the same trophy at the end of the season as the league champions, they begin to become apathetic to the work and discipline that a sport requires to be successful. These kids grow up to become mediocre students and workers. When they reach a point in their education, like college, where they are expected to study and work for their grades, they begin to struggle. They aren't equipped with the coping mechanisms that are required to handle adversity. The same thing happens when they begin working. You could have a group of 35 people with staggered performances and the employee who ranks 21st will be upset because they didn't get assigned a special task like their coworker who ranks 3rd. They expect something for nothing because that's what has been ingrained into them since they started playing in buddy leagues at the age of five years old. The late Dean Smith, legendary basketball coach of the University of North Carolina Tarheels once said "Basketball is a team game. But that doesn't mean all five players should have the same amount of shots." That is the message that needs to be taken away from this section. As much as we are taught that all men are created equal, that doesn't necessarily translate into sports.

Giving trophies to losers is far from the only problem with sports today. Whether we like it or not, athletes will continue to be role models for our youth. And even when those athletes appear to be the role models we want for our children, there is still always someone there complain.

In the middle of the 2015 NFL season, a woman from TN attended a Carolina Panthers/Tennessee Titans game in Nashville. She then proceeded to write a lengthy letter complaining directly to Cam Newton, the Carolina quarterback, for his end zone celebrations, which was published in *The Charlotte Observer*. She proceeded to describe his dances "the pelvic thrusts, arrogant struts and the 'in your face' taunting of both the Titans' players and fans." She scolded him for his behavior and then proceeded to paint a picture in which his actions had caused her fourth grade daughter extra concern and conversation. She states in her letter:

> "My daughter sensed the change immediately – and started asking questions. Won't he get in trouble for doing that? Is he trying to make people mad? Do you think he knows he looks like a spoiled brat?
> I didn't have great answers for her, and honestly, in an effort to minimize your negative

impact and what was otherwise a really fun day, I redirected her attention to the cheerleaders and mascot.

I could tell she was still thinking about it as we boarded a shuttle back to our car. "I guess he doesn't have kids or a Mom at home watching the game."

Now, I don't know how many of you have spent time around fourth graders or have happened to have raised your own children, but those are not phrases a fourth grader uses. Maybe in the middle of English class, they could string together a sentence like that, but it isn't how they talk. It's not normal fourth grade vernacular. If it is for this young lady, then kudos to her and her educators to date, because quite frankly I can't think of more than a handful of adults who would put that much effort into making a comment about an end zone dance...at least not outside of the sports writers who are paid to make fluff pieces about such things. I coached a lot of youth sports and have raised my own son (who two thirds of the way through his sophomore year of high school only has two B's on his record) and I can tell you from my experience, children don't talk like this. These are the views and opinions of an adult.

Her letter received a response directly from Cam Newton, who apologized to her for anything that she deemed offensive. He went on to say he didn't mind her having those views and that everyone is entitled to their own opinion. He responded politely and with all of the respectfulness that could have been asked of any role model.

I however have questions. Why blame it on your daughter? If you're offended, or think you have subjected her to something obscene, why not just say that as a parent you didn't like watching those actions with your young girl? What did you tell her about all of the drunk fans tailgating on the way in and out of the stadium? I know every NFL game I've been to has been inundated with belligerent fans who heckle passersby and can get rowdy enough to throw bottles and other items. What did she explain to her little angel when they were screaming during the game and spilling their beer because they were too intoxicated to care? Has she never been to an NFL game herself? Have she and her family never watched a game on television? Cam Newton's end zone celebrations were nothing new in what was Week 9 of the NFL season. And I guess my biggest question would have been, would she have cared at all if he had played for her team? My gut says, no, she wouldn't.

Not all athletes are worthy of our praise. Between the seemingly endless number of players brought up on possession charges, the night club brawls, domestic violence and even some that garner shame with their antics on the field or court, it's hard to find someone to look up to in today's sports world. So it doesn't help when you get players that act like toddlers because of their lot in life as an athlete.

Jonathan Martin is an example. Here is a six foot five, 327 pound, 26 year old man who claimed to be bullied to the point by his teammates that he quit the team and checked into a mental health facility. Now, you mean to tell me that in all of his years playing football up to that point he had never been engaged in any kind of trash talk? He played his college days at Stanford. I know D-I football players like their smack before, during and after a game. I have a hard time believing that this was something he couldn't deal with. But, sometimes it seems these prophecies are self-fulfilling. Most of the comments made to him by his teammates either stated or alluded to him being a pussy. I guess they were right, after all. I don't condone bullying, but I hardly think that it can be considered bullying when you're a professional athlete and you have some words with your teammates.

Another example of someone you shouldn't let your children watch is Everton Luiz of the Partizan Belgrade, a Serbian professional soccer team. In February 2017, he left the field in tears because of what was described as "horrific racial abuse". Once again, we're not talking about a child here. This is a twenty-eight year old man, playing a sport for a living. I don't know what they said to him, but what kind of professional (or collegiate for that matter) athlete listens to what the crowd says? What kind of sensitive daisy is this guy that he can't take a little verbal abuse from the stands? If he played for any of the teams in New York he'd be run out of town by his own fans, let alone opposing teams.

I bring up these two fellows to illustrate how these kids are growing up now. The kids that were given medals for every project they participated in. The kids that were given a ribbon at the conclusion of every race. The kids that received a trophy for participation that was the same size as the one the league champions received. They are growing up. They are in their mid-to-late twenties, or even a little bit older. They have children now and expect them to excel in every aspect of their lives without struggle or defeat. They believe everyone deserves a trophy and that no one is a loser.

This is why when a coach in Connecticut attempted to curb reports of bullying on his team by making the offender run laps, he was suspended by the league board and subsequently fired by a unanimous vote. He was questioned by league officials asking "...why did you feel you were qualified to handle this bullying incident?" to which he replied "Because I'm a father." He has since removed his two sons from playing in the league as he says it seemed the message to him was that bullying is ok. This is why teachers can't reprimand their students anymore...fear of sanctions toward their livelihood. Most youth coaching jobs aren't paid positions, so this coach and father can take a stand and have small repercussions in his life outside of the football league. However, if the same thing happened because a teacher intervened with similar behavior in the classroom, that teacher could be suspended or fired and jeopardize their entire career.

I was watching a television show just last night that depicted a scene where a girl was in anaphylactic shock on the floor of the school. Everyone was crowded around watching when a mother who knew the child carried an epi-pen knelt beside her, pulled it from the girl's backpack and administered it in her leg. All the while a staff member of the school was standing over the girl, yelling at the mother not to use it because they had to wait for a school nurse to administer any medication. These are the type of things that should be common sense. But in today's world, you apparently can't use common sense without fear of a lawsuit.

The overprotective parents can be found in all activities that children participate in, but they tend to gain higher visibility in sports due to the frenzied nature of their extreme actions. I have said it before, and I will say it again. The worst part about coaching youth sports is the parents. Most of the time, the kids are great. They are kids. Most are eager to learn and have fun and will take direction as needed. Their parents, however, have not learned the same courtesy. They want their child to play a certain position, or have a certain amount of playing time or play for a particular coach.

There are documented cases in schools who held tryouts where the coach and or school were sued when a child didn't make the squad. Who thinks like that? Who has a child that doesn't make the cheerleading squad and determines that it is a matter for the court system to sort out?

For every radical case involving a school board or the legal system, there seems to be just as many that escalate to violence or the threat thereof. In Mt. Pleasant, Pennsylvania a youth football league cancelled their entire season due to threats against league officials. The entire 2015 season was cancelled after shotgun shells were left at the field with some league officers' names written on them. Who thinks that kind of behavior is acceptable? I mean, I get passionate about my sports, but I have never considered leaving threatening objects laying at the field. What kind of person does that?

Maybe the same kind that would cheat at a youth event just to get a win. In Rhode Island, a coach was fired and his team kicked out of their football league when he let the older brother of one of his players play on the middle school team. Some of the clues that were noticed by the opposing team were the boy's tattoos and facial hair. You've got rec league basketball teams that are divided by grade who will take a 5th grader and place them on a 4th grade team just to get the easy win.

I heard from one parent who has a son on a bowling team. The league uses averages and handicaps along with pins to determine scoring. There are coaches who will record scores lower than what the kids are bowling, just to raise their handicap. Then when they enter a tournament with an average of 100-112 and bowl over 150 each round, in addition to getting their 96 handicap they get bonuses for bowling above their average. We're not talking about men here who are trying to con their buddies out of a buying the first round. This is a group of thirteen to fifteen year old kids. Ironically, this occurred in a Pennsylvania league that also began the high school bowling regional tournament by announcing to parents that the coaches are there for a reason and they are to stay back and watch, but no coaching is to be done from the spectators. Maybe they were concerned the parents would find out the real scores the kids were putting up?

So, to alleviate stress among parents and youth, many leagues are now built for everyone to win. So much so that if a team begins to rise above, they may be asked to leave. In Minnesota a girls basketball team was kicked out of the Northwest Suburban Basketball League due to their skill level. A letter was sent to parents informing them that multiple teams were going to refuse to play against them because of the eminent outcome. So now you're telling these girls who went out and tried to become better players, that they aren't allowed to play at all because they're too good. What message does that send to any child that hears the story?

I guess that's why we're up to 40 college football bowl games and have even sunk to inviting teams with a losing regular season record. At the conclusion of the 2015 season, there were 3 teams that went to bowl games with a 5-7 record. Now, there are only 128 Division I football programs. So that means that 80 of them went to a bowl game. Why would anyone not associated with the school directly, have any desire to watch a game between a 5-7 team and a 6-6 team? Why do we need a bowl that begins at 11am on the day after Christmas? We don't. Some of these games have less than 15,000 spectators in attendance, which is well below the average home game statistics for most Division I teams. I know that a large portion of the bowl game picture is that it's about the money. The bowl industry provides a nice chunk of change to the schools who attend and gives those schools one last ditch effort to peddle some merchandise before the season officially comes to a close. I get that. I really do. But to have losing teams play goes beyond the boundaries of logic. There is no reason for 40 bowl games. Up until 1989 there were only eight. It was considered an honor and a privilege to play in one and those schools were considered the top of the line. While the bottom line is money for the schools and programs, it gives all outward appearances to spectators that it's done because every team wants to go to a bowl. If you want your program to be invited to a bowl game, win more games. You shouldn't get in because you rank 79th in the country in your division.

NCAA basketball is edging toward the same problem. The March Madness tournament grows seemingly every other season. There are now 68 teams invited to the "Big Dance" because somewhere along the way they felt like 64 teams weren't giving everyone a fair chance. I'm here to tell you, if you rank 65th in the nation or are considered by polls to be the 65th best team, you don't deserve to go to the post-season. And I'm not even going to get into the NIT and other post-season tournaments that have cropped up in the past few years. Basketball hasn't reached the same level of excess as football, but it's working on it. There are 347 college basketball teams and there are now over a hundred of them going to a tournament.

Youth leagues look to the leaders of their sport to set the tone. It's hard for them to say only the top 6 or 8 teams advance when the NCAA is sending two thirds of their squads to a post-season. Can miracles happen? Sure. But I don't believe the possibility of one occurring should necessitate the watering down of a post-season tournament and or championship.

I think there is hope for future generations, though. As I pointed out early with James Harrison and a few others, professionals and coaches have begun to take a stand and or discuss the issues in public. At the close of the 2016 basketball season, Southern Methodist University's women's coach, Rhonda Rompola, resigned because she felt, "Kids are not as coachable as they were years ago," she went on to say:

"I see kids sometimes talking back to their coaches and it's like a way of life. I'm just being honest. The rules and everything they get, they haven't taken time to appreciate. I was happy to have a scholarship. Kids nowadays are more concerned about when their next cost-of-attendance check is. It's just a different world."

She was the coach there for twenty five seasons.

One of biggest stars in major league baseball over the past few seasons, and the National League MVP in 2015, Bryce Harper, RF for the Washington Nationals, met with a group of Little League players and coaches and while speaking to them he was quoted as saying:

"As much as they might tell you, 'It's OK you guys lost today,' no Johnny. No participation trophies, OK? First place only, alright?"

We have to do something as a society to stop coddling our children to adulthood. If we don't, the ramifications are going to be severe and, I'm afraid, largely irreversible. With the help of stars and coaches like these, maybe we can regain control of our youth sports and go back to teaching the fundamentals of the games instead of teaching children to just have fun and it's ok to be mediocre or bad. The sports generate the passion the children need on their own. You don't have to tell them to have fun. Even if they have to work for it, the sports they love will still be loved. If you thought they enjoyed playing youth sports now, how much more do you think they would like it if they learned to earn a victory and how that accomplishment feels?

"We are all born ignorant, but one must work hard to remain stupid."

- Diplomat, Scientist, Inventor, Writer and one of the Founding Fathers and co-author of the Declaration of Independence and Constitution, Benjamin Franklin

Schools & the Education System

Everyone wants to make good grades in school. Every parent wants their child to make good grades as well. It is an innate human desire to do well when tested. Teachers face a monumental task when it comes to making sure that our children are equipped with the knowledge they will need to survive outside of the school system when they graduate. Whether it's a collegiate path ahead or a trade school, know the majority of my first book discussed sports at the youth level, but those aren't the only problems I see with the sports world in general. Many of the topics I discussed in *8th Place*

Ribbon have gained national attention in the past couple of years.

One of the topics that I have noticed surface more and more is that of homeschooling. Two sections of society in particular seem to have a growing passion for homeschooling are the group that is having trouble making ends meet and the group that receives criticism or scrutiny for their current parenting skills. Now, my question is if they can't even fully perform the parenting side of their responsibilities, how are they planning to accomplish educating their children as well? Are they just mad at the world and feel like they've been given a shitty draw in life because their education held them back? Do they think that because they have a diploma and couldn't find what they wanted that the diploma is worthless? Maybe the root of the problem is a little closer to home. Maybe they can't find a decent job because they don't really want to work.

There are also those who just let their kids tap out of the school system. The kids aren't even being bullied. They don't have any debilitating diseases to hold them out of school in excess. They just don't like going, so the parents say "ok". What are you teaching this child? From what I can see, you're perpetuating the stereotype of the generation and teaching them that if they don't like something, then they don't have to do it. Or worse, you're adding to their belief that everything that causes them any level of discomfort or stress is wrong and they shouldn't have to experience it. I've had similar discussions with my own son. He wanted to skip school one day because he said he was "too tired". I told him, if I didn't go to work any day that I felt like I was "too tired" then I'd never go, because there is not a day that I am not tired at 5:00 am when the alarm clock starts going off. But, as a functioning member of society, we don't get the luxury of staying home just because we're tired. There are some instances where old phrases like "suck it up" do actually have value.

For those who have other reasons for homeschooling, is it a skewed view of the education system because of the parent's own lack of success that points them in the direction to say that the system isn't worth going through? What has given this generation of parents the idea that they know enough to handle this on their own? And, what about the ones who can't teach their children? They let the internet do it for them. So a person who has worked their entire life to learn how to handle your child and teach them isn't good enough but the internet is? And whom do you think created that curriculum that your child is logging into and attempting to go through? Who is going to help your child when they have questions? Are you going to simply refer them to the internet for that as well? While, as an IT professional I can agree with and use the following statement often "Google is your friend". It should also be noted that you have to do your due diligence when obtaining information from the internet. Anyone can post anything they want and portray it however they want. I cringe every time I hear people say that they "read it on Wikipedia". Do any of them ever stop to realize how those answers were entered into Wikipedia? So if you turn your child loose and have them "teaching" themselves on the web, even if doing a structured curriculum established by a sanctioned school entity, they are still going to have questions. When they go to look up answers for those questions and land on Wikipedia (since it springs to the top in a large percentage of internet searches) and they get the wrong information, who are you going to blame then? For that matter, are you checking to ensure that your child is actually learning any of the information they are being shown? Are you 100% sure that they aren't looking at the question on their pc and then searching for the answer on their smartphone and plugging in whatever they find? There is a reason that the classroom setting works. As I stated in *8th Place Ribbon*, I don't think that all homeschooling households are going to fail, but I also don't believe that every parent who gets the grand plan to homeschool is qualified. It takes more than your disagreement with the current standard to qualify you as an educator for your child.

Contrary to the growing popular belief, you

don't have to homeschool just to feel like you have contributed to your child's education. You can simply add it to what they receive. Imagine the world that would be, where the child is able to gain conventional education compounded with their own personal insights and knowledge gained through experience…what kind of people would those be when they grew up? Oh that's right, they'd be like everyone who is currently 40 or older…

A growing sub-category of homeschooling are those who practice "unschooling." This is a philosophy in which the child dictates their own learning path. While homeschoolers protest the public education system, they still typically follow curriculum guidelines and a traditional schedule. Unschoolers do not. Much of the child's "education" tends to mimic life on the 1800's frontier, where the children help tend the farm and learn as needed to handle the situations in front of them. Now, I remember arguing that I didn't have a practical need to learn trigonometry when I was in high school, but even at the time, I could value the majority of what I was being taught.

It is believed that about ten percent of homeschooled children are unschooled. Studies show that students who are unschooled appear to be drawn to careers that are entrepreneurial or arts-related. Imagine that. You let a kid only learn what they want and they focus on get rich quick schemes and celebrity professions. So when this particular group of self-taught prima donnas gets to adulthood, don't be surprised when they want a job at your company but can't write anything except their name and can't count past 34, because that's how many chickens they had growing up on the farm. Maybe some of them have already hit the workforce and that's the root cause behind stories such as that of Mary Lambright back in December 2015. She was working as a truck driver and attempted to cross a bridge in Indiana that had a posted 6 ton weight limit. She knew the weight limit was only 6 tons but proceeded to drive her loaded truck across anyway. She admitted to not knowing how many pounds that was, when questioned by officers reporting to the scene where her truck caused the bridge to buckle under its weight. It was reported that her truck weighed 30 tons at the time of the accident. Even if she wasn't able to do the simple math in her head to calculate how many pounds were in six tons, wouldn't a truck driver in 2015 be equipped with a cell phone that would have access to the internet? In my opinion, it takes a special kind of stupid to willfully not seek an answer to a simple question.

Who is to say that an unschooled child is actually learning anything at all? Could this not just be a lazy parent's loophole out of taking the child to school and also remaining unaccountable for anything regarding the child's education? Could it simply be a legalized form of child neglect, where the children are left unattended to "learn" on their own? It could. I'm not saying that is what is happening in all unschooling cases, but I bet it happens more than that community would care to admit.

One of the main reasons I continue to discuss homeschooling is the fact that since 2003, the number of children ages 5-17 who are homeschooled has risen over 61%. It is now estimated that approximately 1.7 million children are homeschooled. It's very much part of the millennial entitlement movement. "No one is going to tell me how to raise my children" and other clichés are given as explanations. I know some kids that don't even finish homeschool. How is that possible? What environment are you subjecting your child to that they can't even complete the basic requirements and obtain a G.E.D.? Is it due to demanding conditions that hold the child to unrealistic expectations? Or is it parental apathy that allows the child to dictate what they will or won't do, including school work? I would suspect the latter in more cases than the former. Never underestimate the laziness of human beings when given total control over their situation.

I know that I continue to look down my nose at homeschooling households, but I'm not really sorry about it. I feel that a child's education is almost as important to their well-being as the love and support they receive from their family. I went into detail in my last book about the great number of leaders and scholars that were homeschooled, so I'm not going to relive that again. Suffice it to say that I disagree with the concept and will continue to agree to disagree with those who accept and endorse it. I'm sure there are plenty of homeschooled adults and families out there who are smarter than I, and could give you ten thousand reasons why I am clinging to stereotypes and dismissing their lifestyle choices simply because they don't fall in line with my own. Yes. That's probably fairly accurate. My books, my soapbox. If you want to convince people to force their religious beliefs on their children and/or yank their kids from public schools because you don't think they should read The Scarlet Letter high school or because you let them grow up a shut-in without any friends and they can't seem to make any on their own, then write your own book...this one's mine.

Unfortunately, ridiculous ideas on learning do not end with the students who forego the traditional education system. College students readily petition professors for better grades because they "worked hard" on them. Most college students expect to be catered to by their educators just as they were in high school only to find the harsh truth that college professors expect them to grow up and fend for themselves. But that doesn't deter the students from attempting to continue their ability to coast through life.

The University of Maryland received a list of demands from minority groups on camps demanding a prayer room be designated in every "major" building and a shuttle service be provided to transport students to the Muslim center. At the University of Arizona, not only do they want "safe spaces", but they want segregated spaces for each unique identity group (LGBT, Native American, black, Latino, etc.). Students at Yale protested the English department, accusing the curriculum of being too white and imposing only the writings of white male poets. Not to be outdone, Duquesne University in Pennsylvania has had to defend its decision to allow a Chick-Fil-A franchise on campus property because homosexual students there believe it will infringe on their "safe space". Now, this is a Catholic school, mind you, and the Catholic religion is fairly clear on its stance on homosexuality...which is pretty much, don't do it. So what I want to know is how are these sensitive souls, who are afraid of being persecuted by their peers for being in the LBGTQ community, able to attend classes and learn from professors at a religious university that already condemns them for their personal choices? If they are able to live with the fact that they are getting an education in exchange for putting up with the religious connotations of attending a Catholic university, I'd think they could condone eating a fine chicken sandwich on campus, even if they don't agree with the company's values.

Meanwhile, over at Oberlin College, nearly half the student population signed a petition in 2016 requesting that the lowest possible grade be changed to a "C" so that no student would feel "below average." While grade inflation is certainly not a new development, it has definitely reached new heights (or sunk to new lows, if you will) over the course of the last decade.

In Houston, Texas, a girl tried to pay for her lunch in the school cafeteria with a two dollar bill only to be held by the school on suspicion of passing counterfeit bills and had to wait for the police to show up and verify that the currency was legitimate. On year I put $2 bills in each of my nieces and nephews Christmas cards as a novelty, only to have my own son and one of my nephews questioned in a shopping mall in Lexington, KY because the teller had never seen one before.

While I maintain that a traditional education is the way to go, I suppose some of the ridiculous headlines that continue to make national news don't strengthen my case any. In some cities, just making the Honor Roll is a news story. Are you kidding me? It's not like they had an article about the graduating class and threw in the Valedictorian and Salutatorian. No, this was just during a random 4th six weeks grading period the local paper ran a story listing all of the kids in a particular grade who made Honor Roll. I am all for putting an emphasis on education, and we are proud of our son when he gets his straight A's, but I would never think that it should be an article in the newspaper. But this is what we've come to. Celebrations of any and all achievements to the extremes. So much so, that it continues to breed the entitlement mentality. If you got your name in the paper just for making Honor Roll, surely you deserve something extra special if you get straight A's.

One of my favorite examples of education today (or the lack thereof) used to be back when Jay Leno hosted *The Tonight Show* and did his "Jaywalking" segment. For those unfamiliar with it, Leno would go to the streets of Hollywood and stop people to ask them trivia questions. Typically he would ask two or three questions about science, geography or politics and after the person missed all or most of them, he would ask a pop culture question to which they almost always immediately knew the correct answer. It always illustrated how the majority of people only pay attention to or choose what they wish to remember, as those stopped were either oblivious to current events or didn't remember anything from school. Not all of the questions were from a middle school class, however. Some examples were Jay asking people what it means when someone says they are "taking the 5th" or "what is the Bill of Rights?" When asked what bipartisanship meant, one woman answered "it's like bisexual". When asked when the next presidential election was, one gentleman answered "next month" to which Jay responded "January" and he said yeah. Jay asked the same man who he was voting for, to which he responded "Clinton if he's running." Then when asked how many times he had been president already, the man responded 3 times. Even on the rare occasion that people would answer correctly, they would have to think about it or answer with a tone that indicated they were unsure of their response.

I know a game show isn't exactly the most reliable source to gauge intelligence, but in my opinion it brings out a person's inner self. Take a show like *Family Feud*. Contestants are put on the spot with odd trivia questions and have to think quickly to respond. Some will argue that the tendency is to "freeze up" when responding, but I think it is more along the lines of a Rorschach test and it allows your brain to function without taking the time to second guess yourself. One episode I caught on the Game Show Network featured the question, "Besides a chicken, name a type of bird that people eat." (Wording here could be slightly off, but that is pretty close.) One young woman, probably in her late 20's to early 30's, very quickly and confidently responded "Venison". Everyone clapped and her family cheered her on, while she repeated it. The host simply stared at her and forced her to say it multiple times, in obvious disbelief. Another question, answered by another contestant on the same episode, asked to "Name a United

States city that draws tourists from all over the world". One fellow responded with "Florida". The part of me that wanted to be a teacher way back when died a little bit while watching.

Other game show answers that illustrate how horrid our education system is, include:

Question: Which insect is often found hovering over lakes?
Answer: Crocodile

Question: What kind of dozen is 13?
Answer: Half a dozen

Question: What was the principal language used by the ancient Romans?
Answer: Greek

Question: In which European country is Mount Etna?
Answer: Japan
Follow-up: I did say European country, I can let you try again.
Answer #2: Er...Mexico?

Question: Was the Tyrannosaurus Rex a carnivore or an herbivore?
Answer: No, it was a dinosaur

Question: Which is the largest Spanish-speaking country in the world?
Answer: Barcelona

Question: What is the capital of Italy?

Answer: France
Follow-up: France is another country. Try again.
Answer #2: Oh, um, Benidorm

Question: Name something people believe in but cannot see
Answer: Hitler
Question: In which country is the Parthenon?
Answer: Sorry, I don't know
Follow-up: Just guess a country
Answer #2: Paris

Question: Which classical composer became deaf in later life: Ludwig van...
Answer: Van Gogh

Question: Who painted the ceiling of the Sistine Chapel?
Answer: Leonardo DiCaprio

Question: What's 11 squared?
Answer: I don't know
Follow-up: I'll give you a clue. It's two ones with a two in the middle.
Answer #2: Is it five?

Question: What is the past participle of run?
Answer: (silence)
Follow-up: Ok, try it another way. Today I run, yesterday I ...
Answer #2: Walked

Question: What is the world's largest continent?
Answer: The Pacific

Question: How long did the Six-Day War between Egypt and Israel last?
Answer: Fourteen days

Question: Dizzy Gillespie is famous for playing what?
Answer: Basketball

Question: What is the name given to the condition where the sufferer can fall asleep at any time?
Answer: Nostalgia

Question: What was signed to bring World War I to an end in 1918?
Answer: Magna Carta

Question: What is the nationality of the Pope?
Answer: I think I know that one. Is it Jewish?

Question: What is another name for 'cherrypickers' and 'cheesemongers'?
Answer: Homosexuals

Alright, I got a little carried away there and included way more examples than I intended to, but you get the idea. As I kept finding more, I just couldn't stop, as they all deserved to be seen.

When seeing examples of average adult intelligence such as the above, it is no wonder that as of 2015 the United States ranked 40th in Math, 23rd in literacy and 25th in Science which means that speech from *Newsroom* wasn't that far off. So, I suppose when a group of teenagers browsing a guitar shop see a Union Jack painted on one and they complain about how disgusted they are because the store is selling Confederate flag guitars, it shouldn't really surprise anyone.

This is where the premise behind passing every student and giving grades that are undeserved comes back to bite everyone. Maybe instead of focusing on teaching a standardized test, schools should go back to teaching subjects and lessons. Teaching tests only gets a student through that test. They do not retain what they pick up unless they have an identic memory. Teaching subjects, however, provides context and is retained at a much higher rate. It's part of the reason that Common Core doesn't work. Common Core standards create an environment in which tests are no longer a means to measure progress, but rather an end result. In some cases, it actually inhibits a student's ability to grasp and learn a subject as compared to standard teachings of the past. Many college professors agree that the Common Core math standards do little to prepare a student for the arithmetic required for advanced science and engineering programs.

Unfortunately, however, people don't seem to use their best judgment anymore. Sometimes it's a teacher, sometimes a district or county and sometimes it's something handed down from the state level. Wherever it comes from, something needs to be done before we are living in the society depicted in the movie *Idiocracy*.

The number of seventeen year olds who read nothing (unless required by school) has doubled in the past 30 years. And, more than 40% of Americans under 44 did not read a single book (fiction or non-fiction) over the course of an entire year. While the data has surely changed by now, a study by the University of Texas back in 2008 found that 25 percent of public school biology teachers believe that humans and dinosaurs inhabited the earth simultaneously. Eighteen percent of Americans still believe the sun revolves around the earth, according to a Gallop poll.

I can't help but think that one of the biggest drivers of the decline in education is this narcissistic generation of Millennials that have grown up as the political correct era began. The participation trophy mentality leads to a large percentage of them reaching adulthood thinking they are special. "Look at all of these trophies I have, I am awesome!"

Never mind that they are all participation trophies. The legions of Social Justice Warriors (SJW) that patrol the internet have convinced them that they are the center of the universe. Thanks to technology, they have the ability to tell the world every time they eat a croissant or watch a movie.

What is a Social Justice Warrior, you ask? A SJW is someone who attempts to actively solve the perceived social injustices of modern society by organizing within online communities to disseminate propaganda, censor speech, and punish individuals whom they believe should be accountable for these persecutions. Made up of feminists, liberals and radicals, SJWs believe in a societal hierarchy that classifies the level of oppression experienced by each group of people.

Here's an example. If a white man tweeted out that "All Jews are cheap", the backlash would be swift and fatal for his reputation. If a popular gay, black, female said the same thing, nobody would care. The reason is that to the SJWs, the white man is at the top of their privilege chart, while a black woman who is also gay will be granted a larger range of free speech before being viewed as racist. Their "Progressive Stacks" basically say that someone could be a complete moron with idiotic opinions, but because they fall into the right level on the oppression scale, they will be supported by the SJWs and be heard.

SJWs are also the catalyst behind some of the political correctness battles taking place across the nation regarding Native Americans and the schools and sports teams that are named for them. It seems that every few years the debate is resurrected to change the name of the NFL's Washington Redskins. Sportscasters on *ESPN* radio refer to them as the "Washington Racial Slurs" while online petitions call for a name change. Meanwhile, a group who calls itself Redskins Facts, comprised of Native Americans, states that they don't have an issue with the team name and that they feel it is a "proud name"...maybe they haven't watched any games in the past few seasons, but that's another conversation. But, it does bring up an interesting point. Where was the outcry back in the 80's and early 90's when the Redskins were making Super Bowl appearances? Funny how back when the team had a dominant presence in the game, there weren't protests and blackouts and news stories filling your airwaves. Part of that is probably due to the state of technology and information at the fingertips that is available now. But a large part of it is that the Millennials weren't old enough yet to mount a protest. If they had their way, if children today attempted to play cowboys and Indians, they'd be forced to call it livestock management technicians and indigenous peoples. But, who are we kidding, kids today aren't allowed to play with guns or simulate fighting...

It's no surprise to hear that a university in Wisconsin has been asked to remove historic paintings that have hung for over 80 years due to reports that Native American students have found them to be disturbing because they depict a time in their history when their people had land and goods taken from them. Now, these disturbing paintings were of French fur traders and American Indians traveling down the Red Cedar River and a wooden fort with a Native American canoe in front of it. Those are some pretty disturbing images, let me assure you.

Susan Jacoby, author of *The Age of American Unreason*, says in an article in the *Washington Post*, "Dumbness, to paraphrase the late senator Daniel Patrick Moynihan, has been steadily defined downward for several decades, by a combination of heretofore irresistible forces. These include the triumph of video culture over print culture; a disjunction between Americans' rising level of formal education and their shaky grasp of basic geography, science and history; and the fusion of anti-rationalism with anti-intellectualism."

This is why nearly half of Americans between ages 18 and 24 do not think it is necessary to know the location of other countries in which relevant news is being made. Less than 3 percent of public school students tested by the Oklahoma Council of Public Affairs was able to pass a citizenship test, while only about 3.5 % passed by the same survey in Phoenix. And we wonder why reality television has taken over the networks and scripted television and movies all seem to be remakes or reboots or re-imaginations of shows we watched growing up. It's because of two philosophies.

Scenario one is that no one has any original thoughts. Everything worth seeing or hearing has already been seen or heard and in order to relive those moments of greatness, one must rehash old material.

Scenario two, and I feel that this is the larger of the two, is that the majority of screenwriters are currently in their thirties. This puts them squarely as Millennials who think that they know more than everyone else and can do everything better. The superiority complex held by this group is the only logical explanation for why iconic films, such as *Scarface* or *True Grit*, would need to be updated or modernized. Especially when some of the "updates" simply mean including a diverse cast. How about making a new movie with a diverse cast instead of changing the complexion of an award winning film just to include two additional minority characters? Today's SJWs are not content with accepting that history is just that. Everything has to be updated or removed or banned.

It's that same "political-correctness-above-all" mentality that causes people to become offended on social media just because someone posts a holiday greeting. One local news anchor made, what turned out to be, a mistake when he wished a "Happy Hanukkah on December 6th. He ended up being a victim of what I'll call "Salutation Shaming" when people began criticizing him for not saying Merry Christmas. He posed the best question as a response the following day, which was "...how does me wishing folks a Happy Hanukkah on December 6 have anything to do with anyone's freedom to say Merry Christmas on December 24 & 25?" And that's just it. One doesn't have *anything* to do with the other, but enter social media and everyone is offended.

Ironically, these offended souls are the same ones who cry out against the reading of books such as Ray Bradbury's *Fahrenheit 451* in schools, oblivious to the fact that they have become the dreaded "firemen" from the novel itself. And I bet the school district in Virginia would take offense to being compared to the German SS for banning To Kill A Mockingbird because it contained "too many racial slurs". The masses rise up to call the Nazi regime barbaric and decry their censorship and book burnings, all the while staging protests at their local high school because they use a crusader as their mascot or have the senior English class read *The Scarlet Letter*.

The ridiculousness of college censorship has reached epic proportions as law professors have been asked not to teach rape law or use the term "violate" as it may cause students to be uncomfortable. Comedians have all but stopped performing at college campuses, which at one time made up a large percentage of their tour dates. It is considered a microaggression to ask an Asian-American or Latino-American "where were you born?" because it implies that he or she is not a real American. Other examples of phrases that have been flagged as microaggressions (at least in California) include "America is the land of opportunity" and "I believe the most qualified person should get the job."

In 2014, a survey conducted by the American College Health Association showed that 54 percent of college students surveyed said they had "felt overwhelming anxiety" in the past twelve months, up from 49 percent five years earlier. I can't help but believe that our current philosophy of overprotection at all costs and the avoidance of confrontation has led these young adults to a place where they are unable to fend for themselves because they haven't been given the skills to deal with real world situations and adversity. The problem now is by our universities teaching students that their emotions are effective weapons, they are in effect teaching them to nurture a level of hypersensitivity that will continue to lead them into countless conflicts once they have left their "safe space" collegiate confines.

"In reality they all lived in a kind of hieroglyphic world, where the real thing was never said or done or even thought, but only represented by a set of arbitrary signs."

- From her 1921 book, The Age of Innocence, American-born novelist and first female recipient of the Pulitzer Prize, Edith Wharton

The Workplace & Merchandising

If you want to find examples of our society's decline beyond the school system, you can look around at your place of employment and probably see more than you would ever care to see. You see, the kids who have grown up with participation trophies have entered the workforce. They want jobs that pay them handsomely for little to no responsibility. Not only that, but they also want to be handed those jobs on a platter instead of earning them with skills and merit like we used to in the good ole days.

In my opinion, one of the biggest examples of this is the "Fight for 15" fast food workers who are trying to get the minimum wage raised to $15 an hour. When did minimum wage become a destination career? When I worked fast food I made $3.35 an hour back in 1988. Granted, much has changed since then. But, I got paid fairly for what the job was. This is part of the entitlement mentality driving these arguments for higher wages. Fast food work is still fast food work. Outside of management, those jobs were always comprised of high school and college kids. Probably 80% or more. Minimum wage jobs should still be taken for what they are. These are jobs that require little to no skill…training, yes…but "skill", no. I'm not saying that you don't work hard at a minimum wage job, but if a 16 year old kid can do it, quite frankly, anyone can. Why do the minimum wage workers feel they deserve as much compensation as someone with a college degree? I've interviewed candidates for professional positions that carried a 1.4 GPA in high school, so I don't feel that education should be a crutch.

There are multiple avenues for furthering one's education that could provide a desirable labor skill to secure a position that would garner a wage higher than the minimum. Statistics aren't finalized from 2015 at the time of this writing, but in 2014, only about 1.3 million Americans earned exactly the federal minimum wage. Looking back to that same timeframe, in Dec 2014, there were over 119 million workers in the United States. So that's less than 2% of the workforce. The number of 1.3 million was for the federal minimum wage and does not take into account the various state minimums that could be higher, but still be a minimum wage job. Let's say that the number is double when you put those into play. I understand that finding a decent job is hard. Sometimes, it's seemingly impossible. But most Americans continue to strive toward that goal. Not all are successful. But just because you weren't successful in securing a higher paying job doesn't mean that you deserve more for the minimum wage job you have. This is where the entitlement issues come into play. Today's society feels like it deserves certain things. Creature comforts that are in truth a luxury, are viewed by many as necessity. Sour grapes become prevalent as they commute to work and see seemingly everyone on the bus or subway, using a smartphone or tablet. Their children attend public schools where 6 year olds have iPhones and the majority of the class are dressed from top to bottom in American Eagle or Hollister. I understand the place where the sour grapes come from. But just because others have those things, those opportunities, or simply choose to spend their money in that fashion, doesn't mean that you deserve it just because you work hard at your job at

McDonald's.

During one of the "Fight for 15" protests held in Detroit, one protestor was asked by a reporter why she felt she deserved $15 an hour when paramedics who save lives didn't even make that much. Her response was that they "do too much." So the fact that she made whatever life choices that led her to a fast food position in her late 20's entitles her to $15 an hour? It seems incomprehensible to me that someone working a drive-thru at a fast food restaurant could think that they deserve within a dollar per hour as a teacher starting out in 23 states (based on starting salaries at the time of this writing). What exactly gives them that right? They say it's because they can't live on minimum wage. That's your own personal problem. I have known families who owned their house, a car, and raised children on a single income of less than $30,000 a year.

Would I want to do it? Absolutely not. But it is my belief you have to earn a living. If you aren't getting enough hours at your minimum wage job, maybe you'll have to get a second one to secure the 40 hours you need to bring home a full salary. You do realize that the vast majority of positions that pay $15 or more an hour require you to work 40+ hours a week, don't you? So don't complain about how you can't live on your wages at Taco Bell working 26 hours a week for minimum wage. Also, there are enough programs available to those who want to better themselves and their lives, but no one wants to put in the work it requires to obtain the education or skills. They would rather protest their local burger joint because they are only paying $9.50 an hour.

One thing I don't understand is why do they continue to accept these jobs that are so unfairly compensating them? Could it be that deep down in places they don't talk about with their friends, that they realize they don't actually possess the skills or talent to secure a professional position? Could it be that they are victims of social media hype and think they deserve more money just because they read an article where some idiot said they did?

I think there is a combination of reasons behind it. The truth of the matter is that not everyone was born to be a scientist or doctor. Not everyone has the negotiating skills necessary to be a lawyer or the talent to be a professional athlete. Of course, everyone has their excuses as to why they aren't in one of those high profile, glamorous jobs. But the old saying "the world needs ditch diggers too" still applies. You didn't have to take the job working the fryers or the grill.

The "Fight for 15" supporters not only wanted the bump in minimum wage, but also union rights and, to me, that is another group of assholes who acts entirely too entitled.

I don't doubt the need and importance of unions in the early to mid-1900's. But there is no place for them today. Today we have laws that govern how an employer can treat its employees. We don't need a union to tell us. It has been my experience that the majority of union business is in fact, nothing more than the blocking or attempting to block normal work from being performed.

I have never been a part of a union, but I worked at a steel mill where a union was present. It was my observation that the workers spent so much time worrying about making sure they got credit for working a different machine for fifteen minutes at a higher pay rate, that they could have been a more productive and more valuable employees had they just performed their job. The union steward spent more time complaining to management than he did working at the position to which he was assigned. And none of the complaints were anything that required someone's full dedication. "John worked the #1 position on machine 5 for 45 minutes and he was supposed to have worked it for 90 minutes, but Fred bumped him from the spot and he had to go back to the #2 position." That type of shit. All while they were getting paid more while off on jury duty than I did at my regular hourly rate.

I have heard firsthand accounts from government employees who were unable to move furniture (from a moving a desk to switching what side of the desk your monitor sits on) as it violates union rules. They instead must call and schedule someone to come do it, even though they could have done it in seconds. Meanwhile, they have to wait for hours or days for someone to be able to schedule time to make it to their office to accommodate the request.

That's not the only reason I'm against unions, but it certainly doesn't help their case in my eyes. One of the reasons is because non-union members have to foot the bill for union shenanigans in a lot of places. In 2015, a full-time teacher in Pennsylvania had to pay the union $374 for what is called a "fair share fee", even though they weren't a part of the union. California teachers are still fighting in court to prevent their own "fair share fees". It's because of situations like this that "Right to Work" laws have to exist. And they shouldn't. You shouldn't have to make a law that says the union can't force you into anything, because the unions should never be empowered to force you in the first place. Money collected from "fair share fees" is used for collective bargaining and representational activities of the union for all members of the bargaining unit.

The notion that seniority should be the end-all-be-all is another problem that the unions routinely perpetuate. When a position comes available, a job posting is announced. An interviewing panel meets with prospective candidates and decides on the choice that they feel best meets the qualifications and position and awards the job. Then, someone complains to the union, like they are in elementary school. Let's call our offended employee Melanie.

Melanie tells the union, "Patty shouldn't have got that position, I've been here at the company for three weeks longer than her and I think I should have been selected." Now, Melanie didn't interview for the position or even apply, but the union now takes up their sword of red tape and delays the job posting from being filled on Melanie's behalf. Meanwhile, the department who had hoped to fill their vacancy has to suffer through being short staffed and over worked while the bureaucracy fights with the union to determine if they are allowed to hire the individual they wanted to hire for the position they are trying to fill.

Many people who aren't in a union, choose not to be because they don't believe in what the union stands for or what they represent. To force them to pay fees that support the union should be outlawed. If you're a blind sheep following the crowd and or ignorant enough to believe you need to be in a union, that's your right. But keep your union fees to yourself. Because when you decide to go on strike because the company bought a non-union brand of toilet paper, I don't want to have to pay for your dumb ass to sit on the roadside with a sign that reads "Shame on ____" while you collect strike pay to sit all day while I continue to do my job. I have a message for the folks who sit at construction sites and beside busy highways with these signs. You aren't making anyone want to choose a union shop with this behavior. If anything, it makes me detest you even more. I see these folks and say "look, unemployed people". If you want businesses to hire union, provide a quality service and quit asking for ridiculous salaries and conditions. You want to win the job? Bid lower than your competitors. Regardless of what you think you should be entitled to as a union member, business still works the same way. Cost effectiveness will win out in the long run as long as the quality is there.

Prevailing Wage is equally as absurd as "Right To Work". Why is this even a thing? At least I understand why the Right to Work laws exist. They are preventing people from being forced into Union agreements, etc. I don't think the unions should have the power they do, and therefore we shouldn't have to make laws to hold them back, but at least that part I understand. With Prevailing Wage, it's like being forced into a union anyway, even if you're not in one. Isn't the prevailing wage concept the same as minimum wage? There's a reason that minimum wage doesn't have categories by profession. It's because it's a minimum wage. Period. If you are doing something that requires a certain skill set, then you get paid accordingly. Why is a prevailing wage needed? Shouldn't common sense play a factor in what job you take? If you are looking for a job to pay a certain wage, and you have a specific skill set that would dictate that wage, no one is forcing you to take the job paying less. Use your better judgment. Don't take the job anyway and then complain about the pay. You took the job of your own volition. I can't imagine a scenario in which the employer didn't tell you up front what you were going to be paid, so it's not like you were tricked into employment. If you live in an area that doesn't have a position paying what you require/desire for your skillset, you may have to move or change your expectations, possibly even your field. Don't agree to something and then expect your new employer to change just because you didn't get the job you hoped you'd find. They posted the job and you accepted. If you don't accept, and the next candidate doesn't accept, and so on, then they will eventually get the hint that they aren't paying enough for the position and will adjust their offer. I have watched this with my own company over the course of a few years. If your turnover is high, and all of your employees are leaving to go to the same competitor, there's a good chance they are paying better, or offering better benefits. The job market adapts to fulfill its needs when this occurs.

But unions are the only ridiculous things found in today's workplace. We have a workforce now that takes no responsibility for their actions or themselves. I have witnessed in my own workplace employees who won't even call in for themselves, but rather have their parents or spouse do it. We're not talking about someone who was laid up with a heart attack or in a car wreck or otherwise incapacitated. Just an average run-of-the-mill "he's not feeling well" excuse. Trust me, I know that calling off when you aren't really sick has been around for decades, but it seems that people are sinking to new lows to achieve this level of laziness. I get that text messages and email are signs of the times and have replaced an old-fashioned phone call in many scenarios. But calling in to work should still require a phone call. If you are attempting to play hooky, you should at least have to go through the "hassle" of having a conversation with your supervisor to request the day off. There's something to be said for those who possess the ability to feign sickness over the phone. It's a lost art.

Should you happen to have a union-free business, that certainly doesn't preclude you from ridiculous demands. Enter social media and public opinion.

One of the biggest storylines of 2015 involved the confederate flag and its removal from online retailers, and as fallout from this, merchandise from the series *The Dukes of Hazzard*. Deeming it a symbol of hate and oppression, Amazon, eBay and other online giants removed all confederate flag merchandise from their sites. The catalyst for the ban stemmed from controversy surrounding the flag and its use by state and local government facilities, such as the South Carolina Statehouse. For the record, I do not support the Confederate flag or its use by individuals, but now, thirty years after it left the air, a campy television series had to pull it biggest sales object due to public protest. And for what reason? Because some people find the representation of the Confederate flag on the roof of the car, the *General Lee* (which could be argued as the biggest reason anyone ever watched the series, besides Daisy and her cut-off shorts) offensive. What I found to be ironic about the entire merchandising ban was that while they crusaded to remove the Confederate flag, they left the flag of Nazi Germany alone. I don't think there is a more convincing symbol of hate and oppression or one that is as universally known. But it didn't offend the right set of people to garner a retail ban on swastika merchandise. In fact, as I write this in 2017 I can still find swastika jewelry, clothing and assorted other items on Amazon, while the only items portraying the Confederate flag that are still for sale are books.

Along same lines, a home owners association in Utah fined a family for flying the American flag. While I understand that if you agree to join a homeowner's association or move into a neighborhood where one is required, then that part is on you. The fine came during the month of July, in which the HOA dispatched letters to residents asking each to remove all exterior decorations from their homes within 10 days of a holiday. One family continued to proudly fly her American flag which resulted in a $75 fine. How is our country's flag considered to be only a holiday decoration?

Starbucks has caught flack for several years now, because their holiday cups feature their logo on first a plain red cup, then a cup with snowflakes, pine trees and other winter themed images. The controversy comes from radical Christian groups who are outraged that Starbucks won't print the words "Merry Christmas" on their cups.

Disney has begun redesigning the attire of their Princesses in an effort to reduce the sex appeal and depict a more empowered female attitude, rather than their traditional costumes. Even to the point of changing the way their actresses dress in the theme parks. Pocahontas, Mulan and Jasmine have all undergone costume redesigns in recent years. When asked why the change, staff have stated that it is an effort to make the characters more closely resemble the culture they represent. Never mind that they now look nothing like the beloved movies that drew the children to them in the first place. Around the same time that these changes occurred, Disney also was rumored to be discontinuing the production of any new merchandise featuring Princess Leia's slave outfit from *Return of the Jedi*, but we've already discussed that controversy.

But simply attempting to comply with public demand isn't enough in today's society. Updating outfits and removing products that are protested won't satisfy the angry masses. In late 2015, after the December release of *Star Wars: The Force Awakens* in theaters, mainstream news outlets promoted a social media controversy over the lack of merchandise featuring the main protagonist in the film, Rey. They argued that because she was a woman, she was being discarded by the promotional department and overlooked by Disney itself. The truth of the matter was that Rey was the focus of the film and the distribution of too much material centered around her would have revealed major plot points that the studio wanted to keep under wraps until the release.

Disney has continued to battle accusations of female oppression and male dominated storylines by producing multiple movies in succession that feature a strong female lead without any hint or need of male companionship. In an attempt to further modernize, they have even introduced their first confirmed homosexual character in their live action adaptation of *Beauty and the Beast*...and of course, the masses complained.

Old Navy attempted to launch a line of toddler clothing that bore what they felt to be inspiring phrases of "Young Aspiring ~~Artist~~ President" and "Young Aspiring ~~Artist~~ Astronaut". However, the social media machine demanded exonerations for artists and decried the line as "discouraging creativity" and insulting to artists everywhere. Don't tell the haters, but I suspect that these were in fact designed by an artist.

Like everything in American society, attempting to "protect" the offended is taken to excess on a regular basis. For example, take a story that hit a few years back in which a school banned a little girl from bringing her Wonder Woman lunchbox to school because it was deemed too violent. A letter from the school to the girl's parents read, "the dress code we have established requests that the children not bring violent images into the building in any fashion – on their clothing (including shoes and socks), backpacks and lunchboxes. We have defined 'violent characters' as those who solve problems using violence. Super heroes certainly fall into that category." Are you fucking kidding me?

A 14 year old in Logan County, WV was arrested after wearing a t-shirt promoting the N.R.A. with a slogan that read "Protect your right" and a rifle on the front. When the boy refused to turn it inside out, police were called and removed the boy from school. Even my own son has been forced to turn his t-shirt inside out at school because it featured a picture of *Halo*'s Master Chief, who happened to be armed with a rifle, and it was a fake gun held by a video game character.

What ever happened to just ignoring something that you don't like? If you don't like a shirt, don't buy it. If you don't care for the message of a television show or movie, don't watch it. If you don't like a musical artist, don't listen to their cd. Apparently these concepts are too abstract for the mainstream these days. Now it's all about stopping someone else from doing something they enjoy, just because you don't like it or agree with it.

"Undisciplined toddlers become obnoxious children who grow into spoiled teenagers and entitled adults."

- American best-selling author and co-writer of The
Nanny Diaries,
Nicola Kraus

Societal Overreactions

When I began entertaining the idea of writing, I never really envisioned it to go this far. I had my little idea for my little youth sports book and that was about it. But as I wrote that first one, and people continued to share articles and stories with me, it became evident that the problems were much more widespread than I had ever given notice.

It seems that every time I turn on the news or read the paper, I am reminded of just how close we are to becoming that mix I joke about between the societies of *Demolition Man* and *Idiocracy*. I expect in the coming years, possibly before my time here has passed, that we will become a civilization that only has one restaurant, no human contact, we are fined for speaking our minds, music is comprised of commercial jingles, scan the barcodes on our arms to check into the doctor or any other official location, wear disposable clothes covered in corporate sponsorship, watch television from a chair with a built-in toilet seat, we'll elect reality and sports celebrities into public office and convict criminals with some hybrid of the Hunger Games arena and the Running Man gauntlet. Laugh if you want, it's already underway. Between the political correctness censors and the overwhelming innate laziness of our younger generations who are glued to a screen at all times, it's coming.

Everyone wants something for nothing, or more often, to blame someone for their own misfortunes. I don't pretend to be telling you anything new here, but who knows, maybe I am. When I see things like the Mariah Carey or NFL running back Reggie Bush suing the St. Louis arena because he ran past the players on the sideline, all the way to the wall and fell on the concrete, it is evident that something has to give somewhere.

But it doesn't help that we have a government who withholds accountability even for those who commit crimes. In August 2016, the Justice Department ruled that a person cannot be held in jail based on their inability to pay bail for a pre-trial release. While I get that there are those who would support this and cite the recovered penal costs of not having to retain prisoners would benefit the affected jail, I don't understand the logic myself. Why are we telling people it's ok to commit a crime? Because that's the message I take away from it. Sure, they are charged and will have a trial, but now you're taking someone and releasing them back into society and just hoping they will show up for their court date? Jail should be a deterrent. It should be a place that no one wants to go. But of late, it seems that it's become more of a government (local, state and federally) funded rehab facility rather than a place of punishment.

I'll jump into another hotbed of controversy and discuss President Donald Trump's campaign promise and actions to deport undocumented immigrants. The criticism and backlash was immediate and vocal. To say that it was a controversial issue is understating it. But I don't understand why there is such outrage from the average American on the subject. The plan was only to target those individuals who were here illegally, or undocumented. Why aren't they documented at this point? Most of the stories that hit national news were about those who had been here for 10+ years and had children, etc. Why are they still here in an undocumented capacity?

One statistic that I always find humorous is the number of undocumented immigrants currently in the United States. The Department of Homeland

Security and Pew Research Center estimate there to be over 11 million. If they are undocumented, how did we arrive at those numbers? I know there the researchers who publish those statistics have formulas they used to make their educated guesses, but it kind of gives you food for thought.

But, if they want to be afforded the same rights as an American citizen, and everyone who is upset wants the same for them, then why have they not taken the steps to remain here legally? I have no sympathy for them or their situations as I feel it is one hundred percent self-induced. Now, to hear social media's stance on the topic I should be labeled as a prejudice asshole for even suggesting they be shown the way out.

While I'm taking the hard line on issues, why are we working so hard to save heroin addicts? I know, there's that target on my back again for being an asshole, but seriously, some things have a way of working themselves out. While I believe in God and the Bible, there's something to be said for Darwinian theories in humans. The current opioid addiction recovery rate without a relapse is less than 50 percent. For heroin, that rate is close to 20 percent. So only twenty percent of heroin addicts remain clean after attempting to stop.

EMS and other first responders have witnessed an increase of overdose cases in the past five years in record numbers. In 2013, in Indianapolis alone, EMS crews administered roughly 625 doses of naloxone, the drug commonly known as Narcan that is used to reverse the effects of an opioid overdose. In 2016, that number rose to over 1800 for that same department. In the state of Ohio, 2003 saw 87 opioid overdose fatalities. In 2016, that number was over 1400…that's not the overdose statistic, that's just the fatalities. Nationwide, the number of drug overdose fatalities was just over 52,000 in 2015.

On August 15th, 2016 in Huntington, WV, 28 heroin overdoses were reported in approximately a four hour span. A batch had been reportedly laced with Fentanyl, a pain medication estimated to be 50 to 100 times stronger than morphine. Local news programs rarely have a day in which they can go without mentioning a heroin related story, whether it be one or more overdose reports or a wreck in which one of the drivers was under opioid influences. They steal anything that isn't bolted down, and rob everyone from convenient stores to pharmacies in an effort to generate enough cash to get their fix satisfied.

These addicts, by their own admission, care about nothing but the next fix. What's worse is they know that each hit could be their last, yet they continue to shoot up without apology. Many have taken to administering their drugs in the parking lots of 24/7 gas stations because they know someone will find them if they overdose. The bad part is when they don't overdose, they take to the streets in their vehicles and terrorize their local neighborhoods who now must remain vigilant of a heroin induced wreck.

What can be done about the growing epidemic of prescription medication addiction and other opioid drug use? My answer isn't popular, but it's simple. Let them overdose. What happens, happens. I have people I've known for 30 years that are probably reading this right now and getting upset. Everyone has their opinions on the topic. Mine is to let nature take its course. I'd rather let the addicts overdose once and for all than to keep having to fund first responders with the means to revive them over and over again. Some police agencies have even taken to the airwaves to warn citizens of contaminated batches of heroin. Fuck that noise, let them have it. Hell, find the source and give it away for free and speed the process up. Am I being judgmental? You're damn right I am. Am I sorry? Absolutely not. The money that has to be wasted on naloxone alone could make a significant impact in locally ran EMS programs, not to mention the time, gas and other expenses that go along with each overdose call.

And now that reports are claiming that addiction is a disease, and we continue to cater to the abusers and give free revival drugs, why is the country up in arms about free healthcare? I mean, why would you want to aid those who chose to put themselves in their situation and not want to help those who are victimized by cancer and other life threatening diseases? What logic do you use to justify spending the money for a junkie who gets high with their partner and drives their van into a parked car with their 4 year old strapped in the back, yet protesting free healthcare that could provide a 34 year old mother of two the ability to have the mastectomy that she needs to beat her breast cancer? Sure, in a perfect world we'd be able to help everyone. But then again, in a perfect world, there wouldn't be addiction problems. I don't see this as judging our neighbors as much as choosing how best to allocate assistance. Help should go to those who didn't have a choice before those who chose their own path.

Sure, you can accuse me of sitting on my high horse and looking down on those who struggle, because I haven't been there and don't have firsthand knowledge of the power of addiction. But the simple truth that no one wants to admit is that each and every person who tries heroin had the choice not to. Each addict started somewhere along the way and had the power to walk away, but didn't. I've never seen heroin, personally. I've never been any place where it was being used, at least not to my knowledge. So, yes, I judge. I ask, why would you subject yourself to a drug that you know is going to become addictive, you know could just as easily kill you as get you high. A drug that you hear plastered all over every news broadcast, national and local. Why would you pick up a needle and say "hey, I think I'll try this today..." ? I can't comprehend the logic behind making that decision. While I don't condone it, at least I can understand the prescription pain killer addictions. You received those from a doctor for what presumably was a legitimate reason at some point in time, but the heroin I'll never understand.

Everyone has their way of coping with what life throws at them. Some turn to drugs. Some create art, write or play music. Life is hard, I agree. I get it. I also understand that people can find peace with their pets or around other animals. But the rising number of ridiculous emotional support animals should give even a veterinarian specializing in the emotional influence of animals pause. Seeing eye dogs have been around since the early 1900's, and are generally accepted as a way of life for many who suffer from blindness. But over the course of the last few years, a new type of service animal has emerged known as an emotional support animal. These animals have their owners demanding the same privileges as those with seeing eye and guide dogs, including accompaniment on airplanes, etc. The problem is that, basically any domesticated animal can be classified as an ESA. There are numerous websites available to register your animal as a certified ESA. These could include anything from puppies to hedgehogs to snakes, pigs and ferrets. I'm sorry, but you're going to have to have more than an online form to convince me that you need your mini pot-bellied pig with you on the airplane to fly to from Pittsburgh to Dallas.

I'm surprised that animal rights activists haven't stepped in to protest this practice claiming some sort of abuse toward the support animals from overstimulation or problems with air travel. These are the same groups that protested Facebook for the removal of April the giraffe's live birth feed as they said it was considered too sexually explicit. Also the same fanatics who shut down a University of St. Thomas "Hump Day" event in which students would have been allowed to pet a camel. Inspired by a popular advertising campaign in which a camel saunters through an office on Wednesday, the student led group cited animal cruelty as one of their reasons for denouncing the event. They also claimed that it was insensitive to people from the Middle East, although no reference in print or otherwise was made to any race or nationality.

While at this point, it probably sounds like a broken record (if you're old enough to remember what that phrase even means), unfortunately, this is what we've come to in America. The exaggerated desire to please everyone leads businesses, news outlets, school districts, and everyone in between, to have so much doubt and reservation driven by the fear of a social media backlash or lawsuit that overcompensated prevention actions are now commonplace.

This oversensitivity to issues also leads to

overreactions of epic proportions. Look at the polarization of sides on the topic of police violence. It is clear that both sides have legitimate complaints, and no matter which side of the fence you make your camp on, the subject brings out a vigorous discussion from everyone. Released at a time when those stories had begun to take a back seat to other issues, Pepsi-Cola published an ad that featured model Kendall Jenner that ends with her approaching a line of policemen in full riot gear and offering him a Pepsi. He drinks it, everyone cheers and they all live happily ever after. The commercial includes a diverse cast who all come together for what would appear to be the drinking of Pepsi. Enter social media. SJWs unite! The hostile response was so swift and so harsh that Pepsi pulled the advertisement after only twenty-four hours on the air. Critics screamed that Pepsi was trivializing the "BlackLivesMatter" movement and the fight against police brutality. They criticized the use of a white privileged model as the conduit for the peace depicted. All Pepsi wanted to do was sell soda. That's their one and only job. Their marketing team is paid to make you think that their soda is the greatest drink on the planet and that it is so good it could prevent a riot. When I saw the commercial itself, I couldn't believe that anyone would complain about it. It is obvious that these offended souls don't spend much time watching commercials these days, or they would see there are plenty of bigger fish to fry.

A middle school student in Trenton, OH received a 10-day suspension for liking a photo of an airsoft gun on Instagram. I'll repeat that so you can let it sink in a little deeper. For liking a photo of an airsoft gun on Instagram. Reports are that when the boy arrived at school the next day he was patted down and promptly dismissed from school. The note sent to his parents about the incident stated the reason for the suspension was "liking a post on social media that indicated potential school violence." The district superintendent released the following statement to the media:

"I assure you that any social media threat will be taken serious, including those who 'like' the post when it potentially endangers the health and safety of students or adversely affects the educational process."

I understand that social media platforms can be used to stage or warn of pending violent actions. I also understand a school's intent to chaperone their students online activity in an effort to look for signs of potential issues. What I don't understand is how a group of individuals, such as a school faculty, who are continually relied upon to make judgment calls, can jump to such ludicrous overreactions as this. For one, the boy is in middle school. Playing with airsoft guns is part of being a middle school boy. My son and his friends would stage large scale outings where 20-30 boys would gather in full tactical gear to have airsoft battles on the weekends. They start with airsoft guns in middle school and graduate to paintball guns in high school. It's just what boys do. Secondly, I'd like to know what kind of violence was being staged with an airsoft gun that was so severe as to warrant suspending a boy for simply liking a picture? If you go to your favorite search engine and search "injuries caused by airsoft guns" you'll find a list of articles about ocular injuries. Was the school afraid that they were going to be ambushed without protective eyewear on hand? I know, now I'm just poking fun. But you can understand why I exaggerate so abundantly. Using this logic means that if I like a picture on social media, then I must ultimately plan to use it maliciously in real life. So if I click 'like' on a picture of a girl with whom I went to high school with, then that must mean that I'm planning to have an affair with her. If you click 'like' on a picture of a new Porsche when you don't own one, you must be planning to steal one. Seem ridiculous enough yet?

A student at Marshall University found himself in a firestorm after making a Tweet on Election night 2016. Making a simple off-color joke turned into a national scandal about the objectification of women when he Tweeted:

"As soon as Trump hits 270 electoral votes I am grabbing the first girl I see by the pussy #MAGA."

The lynch mobs were ready for him the next

day touting the platform of college sexual abuse victims. The University president condemned the Tweet and the sentiments behind it. Why the Hell can't anyone take a joke anymore? This was obviously a college kid's clever play on the *Access Hollywood* interview with Donald Trump that included his similar statement. I understand if it isn't everyone's brand of humor, but that's still what it is...just a joke. A funny one-liner made by a boy in college. Give me a damn break, people. Keep your panties out of a wad and live a little.

Does anyone honestly believe that this boy planned to or went out after the election and assaulted some poor college girl? No. He didn't and he never planned to. He was just like every other man and high school boy makes comments about a woman when they are in the company of their friends. But even that has been denounced as terrible objectification by the media and SJWs. After the *Access Hollywood* clip, President Trump attempted to defend himself stating that it was merely "locker room talk". It turns out the business tycoon has some baggage he's been carrying around for years, but the just of what he said is true. You would be hard pressed to find a group of men or boys (any age past puberty) and not hear them talking about women or girls they know and the obscene things they'd do to them. This isn't a promotion of a "rape culture". This is guys being guys. And yes, there is such a thing. I have been a part of these discussions and comments since I was in middle school and I have never forced anything on a woman. It is, believe it or not, okay to be a man with urges and discuss them with your friends. Contrary to what the SJWs would like you to believe, not every sexual comment or innuendo is a front for some sinister ulterior motive by the commenter. The vast majority of times, it's just a dirty joke and nothing more.

Trust me, I am not trying to trivialize rape. In fact, I think it's about the most heinous crime someone could ever have to experience and I think they should literally cut the genitals off of convicted rapists. None of this bullshit of only 6% of rapists serving jail time. Every conviction should come with a free castration! Like I mentioned earlier, prison should be a place people do not want to go. But I digress...

The overreactions aren't limited just to the media, though. In their efforts to keep their passengers safe, security screeners at the Carnival cruise ship Liberty stopped a couple from boarding for their vacation because the man had a house key in the shape of a gun. Let that sink in for a moment. A house key in the shape of a pistol was a security concern. United Airlines also made the wrong kind of news in 2017 by having a paying customer literally dragged off of a plane to make space for one of their own flight crews. They offered some cash for someone to take a different flight, and when no one wanted to, they decided to randomly bump people from the flight. The overreaction came when flight crews refused to listen to the man's pleas that he needed to remain on that particular flight and then they escalated to airport security who just did their job. To me this is yet another case of someone who didn't want to deal with the adversity of their job, so the put it on someone else's shoulders to resolve. Kind of like the kindergartener in Florida who was arrested because the kindergarten teacher couldn't handle her.

An Oklahoma high school baseball coach was suspended for what is described as a "tickling" incident. The head coach was driving a team bus when several boys held one boy down and tickled him. It was deemed a hazing incident and official reports claim that the boy was "held down by four kids on the team and forcibly fondled." Even the "victim" in this story denied feeling that he was being bullied, hazed or attacked, yet the coach and several players were suspended for the remainder of the 2017 season.

In 2013, Ronald Jackson, from the Dallas area, took away his 12 year old daughter's phone because he had warned her several times to quit sending inappropriate messages and she did not. The daughter had a fit and her mother did too, who was married to a police officer. She called the cops to arrest the father and he spent a night in jail. The case spent two years in court for the judge to finally rule that the father was just parenting the child and found him not guilty. Thankfully the judge apparently had common sense, as everyone else involved lacked any shred. How do things like this even make it to a hearing? Let alone a court date. I understand the power of the almighty dollar, but at some point lawyers need to have some semblance of good judgment and begin refusing these ridiculous charges.

Many of the overreactions we see are routinely induced by the media. Clickbait headlines draw upon a "shock and awe" factor that wouldn't exist otherwise. San Bernardino in 2017 was a good example of this type of false media hype. Headlines designed to provoke public outrage plastered every news outlet about the "school shooting". It wasn't until you heard the full story that you found out that it was simply a shooting that occurred at a school. This wasn't a disgruntled student loading up to take out his classmates. It wasn't a statement being made by a radical group. It was a murder/suicide by an estranged spouse that just happened to take place at school because that's where his wife worked.

Why do clickbait headlines work? Because the average American has an attention span shorter than a goldfish. Studies have shown that since the beginning of the movement that placed the internet in the palm of your hand, the average attention span is close to eight seconds. A goldfish is believed to be able to hold a nine second attention. With the speed in which people move from one topic to another, it's not surprise that Vine rose to popularity featuring 6 second videos. Sensationalized headlines live in the same recesses of intelligence as six second videos. The ubiquity of the practice has caused many long-standing journalism outlets to close shop or consolidate with competitors in an effort to find a foothold in today's market.

Our every move is seemingly videotaped in some capacity. From smartphones to drones, to surveillance cameras and GoPros, no matter where you go, you are likely to be filmed. So be mindful of that as you go about your lives. That last thing you need is to be another asshole on YouTube who got filmed having a hissy fit at a wine bar because you didn't get your complimentary cheese plate refilled quick enough. It's no longer sufficient to document witness accounts of a story, you need to have video evidence to be considered authentic. Unfortunately, it would appear that the average viewer holds little regard for the full details of a story, but would rather here a snippet recorded at the scene and consider it sufficient.

I am reminded of the movie *A Time To Kill* and the scene when the main character has employed a defense psychologist to assist a temporary insanity plea. The good doctor is questioned by the prosecuting attorney who has managed to dig up the fact that the doctor has been formerly charged with statutory rape. The jury hears this and he is immediately discredited. It doesn't matter to them that the full story yields that the girl he was accused of raping was 17 and was his wife of 40+ years.

And that's our reality now. It has to be catchy, provoke emotion and above all else, quick. If you don't meet all of those criteria, no one cares. The current generation of internet consumers and viewers demand instant gratification and quick fixes as opposed to in-depth analysis. The problem is that it has led to a lack of patience and contemplation.

"We are all born ignorant, but one must work hard to remain stupid."

- Diplomat, Scientist, Inventor, Writer and one of the Founding Fathers and co-author of the Declaration of Independence and Constitution, Benjamin Franklin

Suck It Up, Buttercup

What does all of this mean, you may be asking? If you have made it this far, I applaud you for sticking with me. Not only have you proven that you have a longer attention span that a goldfish, but you also apparently share my concern for where we're headed as a nation and society.

I did not coin the phrase "wussification of America". I have heard it mentioned on multiple radio broadcasts as well as on the internet. The first use of the term that I was able to locate dates back to 2001, in an online article written by Matt Labash titled *"What's Wrong with Dodgeball? The New Phys Ed and the Wussification of America"* published by *The*

Weekly Standard. Faith-based comedian Brad Stine released a DVD of his stand-up routine in 2007 simply titled *Wussification*. The next mainstream example of the term was by former governor of Pennsylvania Ed Rendell in a sermon by Rabbi Benjamin Sendrow in 2011 titled *The Wussification of America*.

Then governor Rendell went on to publish a book in 2012 titled *A Nation of Wusses: How America's Leaders Lost the Guts to Make Us Great*. Other books have followed including *The Pussification of America* by An Executive and *In Fifty Years We'll All Be Chicks* by Adam Carolla.

The current culture of our society is so consumed with protecting feelings that it abandons all reason and responsibility. While I have spent a good deal of time blaming Millennials, they are not solely to blame for the state of affairs we are dealing with. They may be more outspoken than other groups, but everyone above the age of 20 shoulders a portion of the blame for where we're at. Although, it becomes hard to defend them in any capacity when you witness scenarios like the following.

Our carpool was stuck in traffic for two hours on an interstate bridge while first responders worked to clear a twelve car accident. When the emergency vehicles tried to get through, they had everyone pull to the sides of the two lane bridge as best they could and drove the ambulances, fire trucks and police vehicles down the center line in a third "lane" that was created by us moving. An hour into our wait a group of 4 vehicles drives down the center lane, each driven by someone who looked to be in their twenties or early thirties at most. One car looked like it had Kevin Federline's fan club, one a young African-American girl driving with her friends. I understand trying to get to your destination. It was a Friday evening at rush hour, everyone wanted to go home. But what gives you the impudence to think that you are more important than the other 40 cars that are pulled over to the side of the road? What level of narcissism do you possess that can drive past everyone with a clear conscience? I can't fathom it, myself. I would have loved to have seen the police that were working the accident stop them and make them wait like everyone else, and then after the accident was cleared, give them a citation before letting them leave the scene.

Has this just been a forty thousand word rant on the good ole days versus the changing times? I don't believe so. I feel that unfortunately, the average American only gives pause to a handful of issues facing them from day to day. The vast majority then wander through life oblivious to the rapid decline in morals as well as traditional values. I'm not talking about having the proverbial white picket fence lifestyle. I'm talking about conveying sound judgment.

Those of us over forty take the blame from the

younger masses for not caring enough about the environment because we forget to bring our reusable shopping bags every time we shop. They've never seen a supermarket use brown paper bags for their groceries. They've never returned milk, soda or beer bottles to the store to be reused. They parade around with their plastic water bottles and look down their noses at those drinking from a fountain. Parents of school children line up each morning and afternoon to drop off their little darlings at the front door to school, while we fondly remember walking the 10 blocks or so every day when we attended. During the summer break, we hit the neighborhood as soon as we awoke each morning and rode our bikes to gather with friends, only to return at supper time in the evening or by dark, whichever came first. If it weren't for the need to eat and make waste, a large portion of teenagers today would never leave their bedroom if they weren't forced to do so.

There are some easy steps that parents can take to begin the process of changing our culture. Our children have grown so dependent on us to micromanage every aspect of their lives that many are left without the ability to perform routine tasks that were taken for granted when we were growing up. Stop packing their lunches for them. Don't run for the car every time you receive a call that they've forgotten something. Let your child do their own homework. Be there to support them, but don't do it for them, you're not helping anyone with that practice.

Dr. John Rosemond, a family psychologist from Virginia and author of at least fourteen parenting books contends that one of the biggest problems is the fact that young couples today revolve their lives around their children. The kids are the center of their universe. He suggests that one of the reasons older generations displayed a deeper level of respect for their elders was because the children were considered secondary to the adults in the family. He explains this by illustrating that most of the problems being experienced with today's youth are the result of them being elevated to a position in which their parents act as if their marriage and family exist because of the kids. He states that the opposite should actually be instilled to the children. They are a product of the marriage and the parents. The children only succeed because of the house, clothes, lifestyle that the parents provide, therefore they should be taught to respect the parents and grandparents for what they have been given. In his syndicated column published on January 1, 2017, Dr. Rosemond states:

> "'Our child is the most important person in our family' is the first step toward raising a child who feels entitled."

I think there is a lot to be said for this logic.

Let's face it, when we were growing up, our parents didn't consult us about every little aspect of our lives. They made decisions for us and we went along with it. Was it always what we wanted? No, but that was when a discussion occurred. Today's parents let their children rule the roost and submit to their every whim. When we were young, anytime there was a dinner for more people than could comfortably gather around the table, the children were sent to a separate table by themselves.

The simplest solution to most of the problems is certainly one of the most politically incorrect, and that is in short, stop trying to protect everyone's feelings. I watched a stand-up comedy act from Australian-born comedian Steve Hughes who summed it up perfectly in his routine by saying:

> "What happens if you say that and someone gets offended? Well, you can be offended. What's wrong with being offended? When did sticks and stones may break my bones stop being relevant? Isn't that what you teach children for God's sake?"

Your feelings are just that…yours. Personally I don't care if what I've written offends you. I'm actually quite certain that a good portion of it probably did. One of the big problems is that everyone fears public outrage so fiercely that it prevents anyone from standing up and voicing concern or opposition. I'm not talking about protesting here. I'm talking about taking control of a situation before it gets out of hand. Be mindful that there is a difference between thinking for yourself and demanding everything to align to your desires. You're never going to be happy with every situation you encounter. Make the most of it and learn how to deal with the adversity rather than dumbing down the rules or process just to make someone else feel good about it.

Stop protesting every single thing you don't like. It's one thing to protest for civil rights, etc. It's entirely another to protest because you didn't like the results of an election or because a restaurant chain didn't use organic hormone-free range chicken in your salad. If you didn't like the results of an election, try harder next time around. It's why we have a democratic election process in place. Not everyone is going to agree, but the majority rules. The way to protest an election is to vote your candidate into office.

You don't have to run for office yourself. You don't even have to go to the voting office to volunteer for your favorite candidate. But be informed. Learn about each candidate instead and their plans, background and beliefs. Don't let the media tell you how to vote. Just make an educated decision before you cast your ballet. Some of the worst candidates that have ever made it to office have done so on simple advertising campaigns. Maybe the incumbent has lost public favor, and all they have to do is promise an alternative and the masses flock to vote for them. This is one of the worst things that anyone can do. You have to give up party lines and look at the issues and the candidates themselves. Just because someone totes a red flag or a blue one doesn't mean they are going to be what you need in office. Use your own opinions based on the facts that you research for yourself.

The vast majority of the population are followers. Be a leader. Demonstrate the change you want to see reflected. Explain it to those who don't understand. Do you know the percentage of people who sit quiet simply because they don't understand an issue? Or who blindly vote for a name they know nothing about because their uncle told them to? Educate your peers. It's amazing what you can accomplish when you set your mind to it.

If you're mad about budget cuts or layoffs in your city or local government, are you willing to give more in the form of a tax or user fee? Do you have valid alternative proposals for the budget cuts? Send them to your local representative. Most local officials live in your neighborhood, take their children to your schools and work a regular day job. You can approach them with your input, I promise. If you aren't willing to pony up some extra dough or have alternative solutions, then shut up. No one else had any better ideas either, and that is why the situation is dire enough to necessitate budget cuts. Life is full of tough choices. Either dig in and help or quit your bitching.

Many of today's problems are driven by the proverbial "root of all evil" itself, money. Why has the Judge Judy mentality taken over our society? Greed. Everyone thinks they are entitled to something. Why to their frivolous lawsuits get entertained by lawyers in the first place? Money. The lawyers don't have anything to lose, their clients will be paying their expenses, so why not? The system is broken at its core. What can stop this out of control mine car from careening down the tracks to certain doom? Steps like the Lawsuit Abuse Reduction Act of 2017 could take great strides toward curbing the ridiculous suits clogging up our court systems. It would put an end to disgruntled viewers suing the Weather Channel because they got the forecast wrong or parents who sue a fast food chain because their inactive children are overweight. Legislation alone won't stop it completely, however. We need more judges to take a stand and throw some of these things out when they cross their desks. We need lawyers to exhibit core values and refuse cases when they are pitched. If enough of these things get shot down maybe our litigious society will be forced to rethink these ideas before taking them down town to their local version of Saul Goodman.

A large portion of the overprotective rules and regulations that govern our school systems are driven by these frivolous lawsuits and unfounded accusations by parents who refuse to take responsibility for their own parenting failures. Couple that with the failed No Child Left Behind Act of 2001 which caused panic amongst school districts nationwide and triggered grade inflation to run rampant. Schools desperate to retain funding began passing students who would have previously been held back. Unfortunately, the grade inflation caught on with the higher education system as well and a study by a Harvard professor in 2013 showed that in a 200 university test case, more than 40 percent of all grades were in the A range. Untenured professors worry that giving low grades will hurt their student evaluations. These kids have been given A's since they began receiving letter grades, so if a professor gives them a B- or below in something, it has to be that the professor has it in for them or doesn't know what they are doing.

Again, there is no magic wand to wave and fix the situation that we're in. It would take a concentrated effort from multiple directions to even begin to chip away at this problem. From middle schools holding back students when deserved to high schools giving accurate grades instead of passing everyone to college professors giving earned marks instead of passing everyone who shows up.

So what can you do to help? Be a responsible adult. Hold your children accountable for their actions and stop giving them participation trophies for putting on a uniform. Teach your children to respect their teachers, their elders and other people's belongings. Teach them to value what they have and work for what they want. When something occurs in your community that you don't care for, find out how or why it occurred and what can be done to prevent it in the future. Don't get lawsuit happy or demand anything from anyone else that you wouldn't accept if it were you.

.Some of the simplest ideas really do make the most sense. There's a reason The Golden Rule has been adopted by every major religion. The most familiar version of the Golden Rule says, "Do unto others as you would have them do unto you." One website called Palatine Hill lists the following iterations:

- Circa 2000 BCE "Do for one who may do for you, That you may cause him thus to do." - The Tale of the Eloquent Peasant 109-110, Ancient Egypt.
- Circa 700 BCE "You shall not take vengeance or bear a grudge against your countrymen. Love your fellow as yourself: I am the LORD." Hebrew Bible
- Circa 600 BCE "That nature only is good when it shall not do unto another whatever is not good for its own self." - Dadistan-i-Dinik 94:5, Zoroastrianism.
- Circa 500 BCE "Whatever is disagreeable to yourself do not do unto others." - Shayast-na-Shayast 13:29, Zoroastrianism
- Circa 500 BCE "Hurt not others in ways that you

yourself would find hurtful." - Udana-Varga 5:18, Buddhism.

- Circa 500 BCE "What you do not want done to yourself, do not do to others." Analects of Confucius 15:24, Confucianism.
- Circa 400 BCE "Do not do to others what would anger you if done to you by others." - Socrates.
- Circa 90 CE "Do to others as you would have them do to you." - Gospel of Luke 6:31, Christianity
- Circa 100 CE "What you would avoid suffering yourself, seek not to impose on others." - Epictetus.
- Circa 750 "Do unto all men as you would wish to have done unto you; and reject for others what you would reject for yourself." - Hadith, Islam.

I don't pretend to have all of the answers. As stated early on in this book, I am an expert of nothing. I am not conceited enough to entertain the notion that I know what I'm doing. I am just trying to bring some topics to the forefront that people don't often discuss openly, or that the average person may view as uncomfortable or offensive. I do this because I think they need to be discussed. If we continue to bury our faces in our mobile devices and ignore everything going on around us, we'll soon find that we've traveled so far off the road to redemption that we may never get back.

CREDITS AND ACKNOWLEDGEMENTS

First and foremost, I'd like to thank comedian Brad Stine for his endorsement to use the "Wussification of America" in the title of this book. He may not have been the first to utter the phrase, but he was the first to get it noticed in a mainstream avenue with his stand-up routine and recordings titled "Wussification" back in 2007. Available on Amazon in Audio CD, DVD and streaming formats.

https://www.amazon.com/s/ref=nb_sb_noss?url=search-alias%3Daps&field-keywords=brad+stine+wussification&rh=i%3Aaps%2Ck%3Abrad+stine+wussification

http://www.immunizeforgood.com/fact-or-fiction/benefits-vs.-risks

http://www.pbs.org/wgbh/pages/frontline/shows/secret/famous/johnson.html

https://arstechnica.com/staff/2005/11/1940/

SHARE YOUR EXPERIENCES

If you have enjoyed this book and have comments or stories of your own that you would like to share with others, please go online to the book's Official Facebook Page.

http://www.facebook.com/wussification

ABOUT THE AUTHOR

Mike Adams is a part-time writer, part-time illustrator/designer, part-time wannabe-Jedi, works full-time at his day job and is a full-time father. Mike's coaching experience include one season of youth basketball, three seasons of minor league baseball and five seasons of youth football. A former education major at Marshall University, he spent seven years as a percussion instructor for the marching band at his high school alma mater.

Mike's first novel was self-published under the title,

8th Place Ribbon: A Generation of Wussies

and is available from your favorite book retailer.